Pedagogy of the Bible

Also by Dale B. Martin
from Westminster John Knox Press:

Sex and the Single Savior: Gender and Sexuality in Biblical Interpretation

Pedagogy of the Bible

An Analysis and Proposal

DALE B. MARTIN

Westminster John Knox Press
LOUISVILLE • LONDON

© 2008 Dale B. Martin

Scripture quotations, unless otherwise indicated, are from the New Revised Standard Version of the Bible, copyright © 1989 by the Division of Christian Education of the National Council of the Churches of Christ in the U.S.A., and used by permission.

Book design by Sharon Adams
Cover design by Mark Abrams

First edition
Published by Westminster John Knox Press
Louisville, Kentucky

This book is printed on acid-free paper that meets the American National Standards Institute Z39.48 standard. ∞

PRINTED IN THE UNITED STATES OF AMERICA

08 09 10 11 12 13 14 15 16 17 — 10 9 8 7 6 5 4 3 2 1

Library of Congress Cataloging-in-Publication Data

Martin, Dale B., 1954–
    Pedagogy of the Bible : an analysis and proposal / Dale B. Martin.—1st ed.
        p. cm.
    Includes bibliographical references and index.
    ISBN 978-0-664-23306-8 (alk. paper)
    1. Bible—Study and teaching.   I. Title.
BS600.3.M323 2008
220.071'1—dc22

                                                    2007049333

For
Kim Martin,
Lane Martin,
and
Ferryn Martin

Contents

Preface and Acknowledgments

Friends of mine have been a bit surprised to learn that I was writing a book about how biblical studies are taught in seminaries and divinity schools. After all, I have never myself held a teaching position in a theological school, having taught throughout my career in arts and sciences faculties in secular colleges and universities. I just say that I've never had children either, but that hasn't stopped me from telling my siblings how to raise theirs.

I am a church person, though, and committed to the life and future of Christian churches. I have a personal interest in the education of the leaders of churches, which to a great extent takes place in seminaries and divinity schools. I also believe, and argue herein, that the general public of our American society needs to be better informed about the nature and use of the Bible, and that this is important even for those people who are not religious. It is embarrassing, for example, how many times our political leaders or members of our courts make completely misinformed and prejudiced statements about "truths" they believe they are deriving simply from "the Bible" or from "our Judeo-Christian tradition." Our churches need better leadership in scriptural interpretation, and our entire culture needs better education about Scripture and its interpretation. This book is one small attempt to argue that radically altering the way theological schools teach biblical studies is one place to begin—for the benefit of our churches and even our broader culture.

I believe I also may bring a particular point of view to this study since I am criticizing the current dominance, as I see it, of historical criticism in the teaching of biblical studies in theological education. I make this argument even though I am myself a historian of the New Testament and early Christianity. I offer a critical assessment of the value of historical criticism *from the inside*, as an expert precisely in that method of study. But I am also a committed Christian with at least an amateur acquaintance with professional theology.

This book is therefore very much my book. It constitutes my own limited perspective. It represents my views, not a universalizing vision of a committee or a faculty or, even less, a research team. I present here just what I have perceived is taking place in theological education in the United States, mainly in Protestant seminaries. The book also represents how I wish things were different. This study should be taken as one intervention in an ongoing discussion—not to say argument—about how ministers and all Christians are and should be educated theologically.

I should also point out that the context I am addressing in this book is that of the theological *school*, about which I believe I know a bit more than what may be taking place in churches. I am told by friends who work in churches that pastors and laypersons are experimenting with different ways of reading the Bible, that they are not necessarily held captive only to historical criticism or the "ancient" meaning of the text. It would not surprise me if that is the case, since I suspect that those who preach regularly from these texts or who desire to use them in their lives devotionally must come up with various meaningful ways to read the Bible. I do believe, though, that formal theological education as practiced in this country could reform itself to allow its curriculum better to meet those needs. And that is the focus of this book.

Another preliminary point that relates to audience: though it may appear that I have in mind mainly theological educators—the professors and administrators who actually run seminaries and divinity schools to a great extent—I hope my audience will include students, prospective students, denominational leaders, ministers, and laypeople. Only with the involvement of all these kinds of people, I'm convinced, will theological education be changed. Many schools, for example, construct their curricula to meet expectations or even requirements put upon them by denominational bodies. These "extra-school" institutional expectations must themselves change in order for curricular structures to change, and that means changing church and denominational cultures and not just schools themselves. I hope this book, therefore, will have a wider readership than merely professors and administrators of schools.

In order to expand my own vision a bit, I visited ten different theological schools, in different parts of the country and representing different theological points of view, from liberal or progressive to conservative or evangelical, and in between. I chose schools of different denominations and no denominational affiliation, schools in major cities and smaller towns, free-standing seminaries and divinity schools connected with major research universities. I am grateful to the ten schools—their administrators, faculty, and students—

who welcomed me and made my study not only more complete but even pleasant. Those schools are:

> Candler School of Theology, Emory University (Atlanta)
> Columbia Theological Seminary (Decatur, Georgia)
> Chicago Theological Seminary (Chicago)
> Fuller Theological Seminary (Pasadena, California)
> Gordon-Conwell Theological Seminary (South Hamilton, Massachusetts)
> Interdenominational Theological Center (Atlanta)
> Lancaster Theological Seminary (Lancaster, Pennsylvania)
> Moravian Theological Seminary (Bethlehem, Pennsylvania)
> North Park Theological Seminary (Chicago)
> The University of Chicago Divinity School (Chicago)

The product of my visits to these schools was transcriptions of ninety-eight interviews of about twenty to thirty minutes each. I interviewed forty-eight instructors and fifty students. I tried to concentrate, though not exclusively, on students in master of divinity programs, that is, those in programs that train mainly people preparing for ordination. I did not follow a rigid questionnaire, but I did generally ask the same questions. I had one set of questions for faculty teaching in biblical studies, slightly different questions for those teaching in other fields, and a different set of questions for students. Besides these individual interviews, I also collected materials, such as syllabuses and course materials, that gave some indication of how biblical studies were taught, and I attended some classes to observe instruction in biblical studies. These personal investigations have been supplemented by published studies on theological education and investigations over the Internet of different schools, their curricula, and course materials. I benefited also from the curricular materials made available on the Web site of the Wabash Center for Teaching and Learning in Theology and Religion.

I realize that my visits to these schools and interviews in no way constitute the gathering of scientific data. It had long been my sense that historical criticism was given deference in the teaching of biblical studies in seminaries and divinity schools in a way that other methods were not. I wanted to see if that was true, or if my perceptions simply stemmed from the fact that I am myself trained as a historical critic. My modest survey of ten different schools—combined with searches of published literature and Internet Web sites for schools and other resources—constituted an attempt to check my sense with concentrated observations. Yet I am not a social scientist and have no desire to represent my work as rising to that level or meeting the expectations of sociological research. My surveys and interviews were pursued simply to enable me to listen to other voices, not to establish some kind of objective scientific data.

People quoted from my interviews have been kept anonymous in the book in many instances—students almost all the time, professors in cases where I felt their comments were for me in confidence, or where I felt that citing their names might cause embarrassment either to them or to their colleagues. All the quotations, though, come from my transcriptions of interviews and are as accurate as I could render them.

This study was made possible by a generous Study Leave Grant from the Wabash Center for Teaching and Learning in Theology and Religion. I am very grateful for the generosity of the Wabash Center—as well as the advice and guidance I received from the personnel of the center about how to pursue the project. I am also grateful to Yale University for granting the research leave for the academic year 2005–2006.

For reading the manuscript and providing important advice, I thank Ken Stone, Kathryn Tanner, Denise Thorpe, Susan R. Garrett, and my sister, Ferryn Martin. I especially wish to thank all those dedicated instructors and students who gave me their valuable time and so openly, generously, and wisely shared with me their experiences of the sometimes precarious journey of theological education.

The book is dedicated to my brothers and sister, from whom I've learned much about love, and therefore about God.

1

The Bible in Theological Education

I grew up in a very Bible-centered church—okay, it was fundamentalist—and was taught a lot of Bible. We knew Bible stories, Bible characters, and memorized many Bible verses. Even now, I need only hear the beginning words of certain verses, especially in the King James Version, and I will finish them automatically. And I don't mean just the "big ones," such as "For God so loved the world . . ." (John 3:16; recognized by any decent football fan who watches TV). We also memorized more obscure passages. Decades later, I can still finish: "Study to show thyself approved unto God . . ." (2 Tim. 2:15); "Repent, and be baptized every one of you . . ." (Acts 2:38); "Go therefore and make disciples of all nations, baptizing them . . ." (Matt. 28:19; for some reason, I learned this one from the Revised Standard Version); and many more. We kids—or at least those of us whose parents herded us to church all the time—knew our Bibles.

Some of us former fundamentalist kids remember "sword drills," popular sometimes in Sunday schools but especially as a competition at Bible camp. We would stand at attention with our Bibles held stiffly at our sides, like clumsy Revolutionary War muskets. The teacher would shout, in her best marine sergeant voice, "Pre-sennnnt ARMS!" and we would snap to attention with our Bibles, our "swords," ready in front of us (". . . and the sword of the Spirit, which is the word of God . . . ," Eph. 6:17). The teacher would call out a Bible book, chapter, and verse ("Jeremiah 21:8!"), and we would race to get there first. The first student who found the passage was supposed to plant a finger on the verse and read it out, loudly. The other kids groaned in jealousy and looked forward to the next drill.

So at least some of us grew to adulthood with much of the Bible pounded into us; whether voluntarily or not was another question. In any case, long before I ever attended seminary, I may not have known much about sophisticated modern methods of interpreting Scripture, but I at least had much of the Bible in my head. And I was not the only one. Not so long ago—recently enough that older professors can remember it well—faculty teaching in seminaries and divinity schools could assume that their beginning students mostly knew their Bibles. Students may not already have been educated in the critical study of Scripture, but they could be expected to recognize basic stories, characters, and phrases from the Bible. In earlier generations in this country, authors could expect most of their readers to recognize titles such as *East of Eden*, *The Power and the Glory*, or *The Grapes of Wrath* as quotations of Scripture. Political speeches could be sprinkled with biblical quotations and allusions with the expectation that many if not all the hearers would not only recognize them as being from the Bible, but might even be able to tell where to find them.

No more. If you ask professors now teaching in theological schools, even those at which students have already been active in churches and are themselves only three years away from assuming full-time jobs as leaders or pastors, instructors will tell you that the level of basic knowledge of what's in the Bible is generally low. They will say that they feel at a disadvantage because they must teach not only how to interpret the Bible, but also basic Bible knowledge that in previous generations—at least according to their perceptions—was carried as cultural equipage by any generally educated citizen, not to mention regular churchgoers.

Thus, the first course in biblical studies that the beginning theological student takes—whether a course in methods for studying the Bible, an "Introduction" to the Old or New Testament, or a course on biblical topics—may in many cases serve as the student's first sustained encounter with Scripture. For the student who in two or three short years may be serving as a minister or even the sole pastor of a congregation, one of the most important and enduring things learned will be scriptural study, including how to read the Bible. What methods of interpretation will be absorbed, either consciously or unconsciously? What sorts of questions will be considered appropriate to put to the text? What kinds of readings will be accepted as "responsible" and what dismissed as "fanciful"—or worse, "dangerous"? Indeed, how will the student learn to conceptualize the very nature of Scripture? What sort of thing is this text? What should we expect to get from it? How should we teach members of our churches to use it?

There is, of course, diversity in how biblical studies are taught in U.S. theological schools. But even a brief survey reveals that almost all postgraduate education in biblical studies, whether in "liberal" and "progressive" or "conservative" and "evangelical" schools, depends heavily on the historical-critical method developed since the nineteenth century. In some schools, this is basically the only method students are thoroughly taught. In others, historical criticism may be supplemented by other ways of reading the text. And in some schools there has been an attempt to de-emphasize the role of historical criticism in order to promote other, sometimes more theologically sensitive, ways of reading Scripture. But the basics of historical criticism, which I explain below, are taught almost everywhere, certainly in all seminaries and divinity schools educating the clergy of major Protestant denominations. One would have to say that in spite of recent innovations and moves away from teaching only historical criticism, that method is still the dominant one taught to students training to be ministers. They may be taught to go beyond the historical meaning of the text, but that historical meaning is nonetheless predominant or foundational in the education of most clergy.

In this book I explain what I mean by "historical criticism," demonstrate its current dominance in American theological education, and urge that we move beyond that dominance. I want to emphasize at the outset, though, that I am not advocating that we jettison historical-critical approaches to Scripture. I just advocate that we dethrone it as the only or foundational method taught, and that we supplement it with other methods, approaches, and theories. Historical criticism may be useful; it need not be king.

WHAT IS HISTORICAL CRITICISM?

Different people mean different things by the term "historical criticism." In this book, "historical criticism" refers to the method of interpreting the Bible that arose mainly in the nineteenth century and was early pursued most vigorously in Germany.[1] For generations, it dominated scholarly interpretation and became, practically, the only way scholars and ministers were taught. Although there was opposition to many of the assumptions, goals, and practices of historical criticism on the part of fundamentalist and conservative Christians and institutions, the most basic assumptions of the historical-critical method came to dominate teaching of Scripture—even in conservative and evangelical Christian schools.

At its most basic level, historical criticism takes the primary meaning of the text to be what its meaning would have been in its original ancient context. For many people, this is what "the author intended" to communicate when writing the document. When the prophet Jeremiah said, "The LORD said to me in the days of King Josiah" (Jer. 3:6), he intended for us to understand that he, Jeremiah, received a message from God while Josiah reigned in Jerusalem and that what follows is the message Jeremiah wants to deliver to the people of Israel. When Paul wrote to the Corinthians, "Be imitators of me, as I am of Christ" (1 Cor. 11:1), he was calling those new followers of Jesus to fashion their behavior on Paul's behavior, which was fashioned on that of Christ. It would be a mistake, from the point of view of historical criticism, to take the "King Josiah" of Jeremiah's text as a reference to Josiah Bumbershoot who owns a liquor store down the street. Why? The text doesn't *say* that it is *not* referring to Mr. Bumbershoot. But historical criticism assumes that the foundational meaning of the text must refer primarily to the time of Jeremiah himself and what Jeremiah wanted to communicate. Historical criticism would similarly reject an interpretation of Paul's statement (that is, *as* a historical-critical interpretation) that took the "me" to refer not to Paul but to *me*, Dale Basil Martin. That could be a way I might use the text for a different purpose, but it would not be acceptable as the historical meaning of the text established by the methods of historical criticism. The primary meaning according to historical criticism is the meaning of the text in its ancient context, either the intentions of the author or the meaning understood by the ancient audience.

That last point, about the ancient audience, in fact points to recent developments within historical criticism itself. Whereas previous generations of scholars tended to focus on the intentions of the author to establish the primary meaning of the text, scholars more recently have recognized the great difficulties we encounter when trying to guess at authors' intentions, especially of authors who wrote two thousand years ago.

In fact, all scholarly claims about an ancient author's intention are guesses, because we could have no conceivable access even to that author, much less to his intentions (and for biblical texts, we tend to assume, probably correctly, that the authors were men). So many scholars and students combine talk about the intentions of the author with talk about what the ancient audience or ancient readers would likely have taken the meaning to be. Thus, for example, the first hearers of Jeremiah's message would naturally have assumed that he was referring to the King Josiah they knew about, and not to some "Josiah" living in the modern world, so that would be the primary, historical meaning of the text. And Paul's readers would have taken his "me" to refer to Paul himself and not to *me*, Dale Basil Martin. The historical-critical meaning of the text must be anchored in the social and cultural realities of the ancient context of the text's production and reception. That is the most basic meaning of the term "historical-critical" when I use it.

Certain techniques are regularly taught to students to train them as historical critics of the Bible. Many of these revolve around the central principle underwriting historical criticism: a historical consciousness of modern people that we live in a different world compared to those who lived before us. Languages, societies, cultures all change through time, sometimes radically. We cannot assume that words that mean one thing for us meant the same for people even two hundred—much less two thousand—years ago. So we must do research to try to ascertain what a text written in a different time and place would have meant then. We cannot assume that it will mean the same for us. This recognition that we and the ancients occupy different cultural worlds is what I mean by "historical consciousness."

Since these texts were composed to be meaningful in the ancient world, in the ancient Near Eastern and Mediterranean worlds to be specific, one starting point for historical criticism is learning as much as we can about those ancient worlds. Students are therefore regularly taught something about ancient Israelite history and society, the ancient Jewish context, and Greco-Roman cultures. Since ideally historical criticism of the Bible should include study of the texts in their original languages, some exposure to Hebrew and Greek is attempted, even if that is no more than teaching students who can't actually read Hebrew or Greek to use English reference books to help them gain some idea of the underlying ancient languages of the Bible. Students therefore are soon introduced to reference books such as analytical concordances, Bible dictionaries, and books that display different English translations side by side. For those students who have learned some Hebrew or Greek, the analysis of grammar is included. But even for those who can use only English, students are taught to outline passages and books, to analyze the structure of the narrative or argument of the text, to identify certain rhetorical devices such as chiasm or parallelism, to recognize different genres of literature, differentiating an analysis of poetry from one of narrative, or noting when a text is presenting a parable rather than a legal argument. How does one interpret a book of prophecy differently from a book of history? At a bit more advanced level, students may be introduced to textual criticism, the practice of comparing different manuscript versions of a text in order to establish which Greek wording represents the most likely "original" writing.

Beyond these rather basic, though indispensable, skills, historical criticism teaches students to read the Bible not as one, unified book, but as a collection of documents written at different times by different people with different needs and goals. One of the fundamental lessons most students are taught in seminary is that they should interpret each document of the canon in its own light rather than through the lens of another part of the Bible. So a psalm should be interpreted, at least to some extent and at some stage, by what it would have meant for its original authors and readers—that is, as a reference to David, or another Jewish king, or the Temple, or Jerusalem—rather than as a reference primarily to Christ or the church. The Gospel of Matthew should be interpreted on its own terms rather than through the lens of the Gospel of John. Students are taught that the portrayal of Jesus in Matthew, for example, may be somewhat different from the portrayal of Jesus in John, and those different portraits should be acknowledged and even honored. Harmonization of different parts of the Bible is taken by historical criticism to be an error, at least at the most fundamental level of historical exegesis. Different documents and authors must be interpreted relatively independently. In courses on Paul, for instance, it is not unusual for the instructor to insist that students even avoid interpreting Galatians through the lens of Romans or vice versa. They are taught that Paul may have been doing rather different things in the two different letters. This interpretive principle embodies a key methodological assumption of modern historical criticism.

But of course, the method also recognizes that the authors of these documents did use other documents as sources for their own writings. The beginning sentences of the Gospel of Luke are held up as obvious evidence that its author knew and used previous Christian sources, both oral and written, for his work. In fact, most scholars teach that both Luke and Matthew used Mark as a primary source for their own Gospels. In scholarship on the Hebrew Bible, students are regularly taught the modern theory that the Pentateuch, the first five books of the Bible, is a compilation of perhaps four different documents or sources, the Yahwist, the Elohist, the Deuteronomic, and the Priestly sources, a theory known as "JEDP" (the German spelling of Yahwist uses an initial "J," and it was Germans who invented and elaborated the theory). New Testament students will often be shown that the author of 2 Peter seems to have used Jude as his main source, editing it to serve his own purposes and to accommodate later Christian sensibilities. The identification of sources and different editorial levels of biblical texts is a fundamental technique of modern historical criticism, and almost all theological students are taught some version of it.

At more "liberal" Christian institutions—that is, those schools and denominations that feel no need to affirm the absolute historical veracity of the Bible—historical-critical techniques will be pressed further than just establishing the probable "original meaning" of the texts. In those schools, students will be taught to question the authorship of biblical books: some of the letters that claim to have been written by Paul seem to have been written by other people, in some cases long after Paul's death. The Pentateuch was certainly not written by Moses but by anonymous authors and editors over a long period of time. The Gospels were probably not written by the persons whose names they carry, but were most likely first published anonymously, only later to have been attributed to apostles and other known followers of Jesus and Paul. Students are also taught to question the literary integrity of some biblical books: Isaiah was not originally one book, but at least two documents, or three, that went through a long editing process and had different authors; 2 Corinthians is almost certainly a compilation of fragments of at least two different letters of Paul, and perhaps as many as five.

Perhaps most disturbing for many students is the idea that the "facts of history" must have been quite different from the way they are portrayed in the Bible. The accounts of the creation, they will be told, are certainly mythological and have no basis in history. The portrait of the growth of the early church presented by the author of Acts is idealistic and idyllic and not a historically accurate picture of the no doubt very messy development of early Christianity. And with four *different* presentations of the activities, death, and resurrection of Jesus, the distance between any of the accounts and what actually happened must be significant. In fact, one of the fundamental principles of the historical-critical method when taught in more "liberal" institutions is the *problem* of the diversity, conflict, and even contradiction within Scripture, with reference both to historical events as well as to doctrine or ethics. True, these sorts of positions may not find much place in more evangelical or conservative schools, but at least questions such as these almost automatically arise within the learning and practice of the historical-critical method.

There are also certain themes that perhaps do not rise fully to the level of a methodological principle but that rule the assumptions about and practice of historical criticism. The great bogeyman of historiography, for example, is anachronism. According to the rules of historical criticism, an interpretation of the text must make sense as understood within the historical context of the text. So attributing a modern concept to a first-century document without demonstrating that the modern concept actually did or conceivably could exist in the first century goes against the assumptions of good historiography. Another assumption is that authors are human beings and products of their own culture and society, so interpretations of their writings should be plausible as products of their culture. Even if a Christian historian believes an author was "inspired," that historian—when behaving *as* a historian—will interpret the text using concepts and categories available to normal human beings of the particular culture (or combination of cultures) of the human author.

Although the term "exegesis" literally means simply "interpretation of a text"—not specifying the method of interpretation—most modern scholars and most students under their influence use the term in the more limited sense of historical interpretation.[2] And just about every seminary student will have been indoctrinated in the idea that the opposite of (good) "exegesis" is (bad) "eisegesis," understood as "reading into the text" meanings that are not truly "in" the text. So "eisegesis" has become the watchword for biased, personally driven interpretations that are the opposite of those produced by "responsible," historically sensitive interpretations. The assumption here is that there is "meaning" inherent in the text needing merely proper excavation to be brought to light. Eisegesis is taken to be the burying of one's own "meaning" in the text, rather than digging out the text's "true meaning."

Finally, we may recall the issue of historical consciousness raised earlier. The historical method has taught modern people to recognize that there exists a "gap" between our own time and ancient times. Ancient cultures and societies were fundamentally different from ours. If we want to understand their languages, concepts, beliefs, or worldviews, we must figure out some way to overcome the gap between their world and ours. This notion of a gap between the past and the present is a fundamental product of modern historical consciousness. Different kinds of schools have different ways of dealing with the gap. Schools, professors, and students who see themselves as more "true to the Bible" than other ("liberal"?) Christians tend to minimize the gap: they just insist that their own assumptions and beliefs are actually not significantly different from those of ancient Christians. Modern Christians who feel less need to defend their practices and beliefs by appeal to what the Bible says, on the other hand, tend to admit a larger gap between their own practices and beliefs and those of ancient Christian writers. But the impact of modern historical consciousness can be seen across the theological spectrum.

For example, more "liberal" Christians may recognize a large gap between their own sexual ethics and those of, say, the apostle Paul. More "conservative" Christians usually want to admit less of a gap between themselves and Paul when it comes to sexual ethics, but they will usually admit something of a gap nonetheless in their insistence, for example, that Paul's instructions in 1 Corinthians 11 that women must veil themselves represents a mere cultural artifact that is not binding on modern Christian women. A gap between Paul's historical situation and ours is taken as a valid reason to reject Paul's instructions as binding for modern Christians, even by "conservative" and "evangelical" Christians. My point here is that Christians of a wide variety of theological dispositions all recognize significant differences between the ancient world and our modern world, and that is a result of the rise of historical consciousness in the modern world and is expressed in the practices of historical criticism of the Bible.

None of my presentation thus far is meant to deny that important differences exist among professors over what precisely counts as "historical criticism." Some professors shy away from the term "historical-critical" and prefer something else, such as "historical-grammatical" or "historical-contextual." Such scholars sometimes see the term "historical-critical" as implying that modern Christians may pass judgment on the content of the Scriptures. Others avoid the term "critical" because they take it to refer to making negative decisions about the historicity of the narratives. Still others avoid the term historical-critical because it makes the subject sound like ancient history, that is, dry or irrelevant. Cynthia Linder at the University of Chicago Divinity

School said of the term, "When I hear that used these days it seems to refer to an emaciated or eviscerated subject. I hear the term used in a disparaging way, and I don't think that is what [the students here] are getting. They are getting historical tools, critical tools. But there are ways in which more is conveyed about what this might mean than just what is in the text historically." Or as Julia O'Brien at Lancaster Theological Seminary said, "I don't use that word much because it is too much of a lightning rod. I prefer to talk about historically grounded readings. You have to understand first that these texts have a history written in a particular context, and interact with political, social contexts."

Still others reject the label "historical-critical" because for them it refers merely to the practice of reconstructing what really happened, using the texts as a mere window onto ancient historical events. The narratives of the exodus, in such a practice, would be read not so much with interests in literary struc- ture or narrative, or for concepts of God and God's people, but merely in order to attempt a reconstruction of what actually happened. To cite another exam- ple, the Gospels would be merely mined for historical facts about the life of Jesus of Nazareth, rather than being appreciated as literary or theological texts in their own right. Almost all scholars today reject this sort of practice, and that is what many instructors are rejecting when they demur from describing their methods as "historical criticism." Gail O'Day, at Emory's Candler School of Theology, for example, noted that some might understand historical criti- cism to mean simply "historical reconstruction" or "reconstructing a particu- lar time line or the history of the early church," practices she herself would de-emphasize. Yet she admitted that she taught students historical criticism, if by that we mean "attending to the context in which the text was written." In spite of different understandings of what historical criticism is, therefore, almost all instructors of biblical studies, across the board theologically and institutionally, practice and teach what I have identified above as basic histor- ical criticism: the use of linguistic and historical analysis to establish the ancient meaning of the language of the biblical texts.

ALTERNATIVES TO HISTORICAL CRITICISM

Many biblical scholars are experimenting with other ways of reading the Bible, introducing their students to a variety of methods, models, and stances for interpreting Scripture. Regularly, instructors emphasize that they concentrate less on teaching content, that is, simply what information is contained in the Bible, and more on process, teaching students how to deal with the text, how to read. As Greg Carey at Lancaster Theological Seminary put it, "The goal of my courses is for students to cultivate their own practices of interpretation and to own their identity as responsible public interpreters of Scripture. I'm not teaching them a bunch of stuff to remember. We do the practice of interpretation together, and that's the process I'm interested in. Process driven rather than content driven, lots of writing, feedback, essays, that sort of thing." Professors at different schools use the term "tools" for the skills they attempt to inculcate in their students. They see the basic skills of traditional historical criticism—original languages if possible, word studies, rhetorical and structural analysis, understanding of ancient culture and context, ascertaining authorship and first audience—as simply tools that should be used along with others for learning to read the text in self-conscious, critical ways.

Others go further, however, and confess to moving away from historical-critical methods, at least to some extent. When asked about the role of historical criticism in her courses, Deborah Appler of Moravian Theological Seminary responded, "Dead white guys. I still teach it, but I spend very little time on it, as almost a historical artifact. I have to confess that the historical-critical method is not so central for me anymore. I'm more interested in how different communities interpret. I'm more on the postmodern side, though I do find the other still important." Stan Saunders, at Columbia Theological Seminary, also found himself moving away from traditional historical criticism:

> I don't know if I teach historical criticism anymore or not. I was educated that way, and I want people to understand the documents in their historical and cultural settings. I see these as good tools. But I wouldn't necessarily describe myself as a historical critic anymore. I want to engender a relationship with the text, give them a set of tools so they can develop their own relationship to the text. I try to encourage them to get some sense of the richness of the material, how varied, textured, and generative for imagination the materials can be. I'm not so interested that they come out with a particular method they are schooled in.

When professors are asked what other approaches or methods of reading Scripture are taught, the most commonly mentioned are literary, feminist, and social-scientific. "Social-scientific" covers several different approaches to reading the Bible that borrow questions, models, or methods from disciplines such as sociology and historical sociology, cultural anthropology, and social history.[3] Feminist approaches may also include a variety of differences, from attempting to discover women and their voices in ancient history or early Christianity; to applying more critical theories of gender and sexuality to biblical issues; to teaching a hermeneutics of suspicion when reading male authors, either those of the Bible or those in the history of interpretation; to simply teaching readers to adopt a feminist point of view in reading. When professors say they teach literary methods, they are usually referring to the analysis of the text by paying attention to structure, plot, characterization, voice, and genre, the sorts of analysis best exemplified by the New Criticism dominant in literature and English departments through the 1950s and 1960s.

In fact, literary and other approaches seem to be emphasized more by Old Testament or Hebrew Bible faculty than by New Testament faculty, perhaps because there is simply so much more literature and varieties of literature in the Old Testament—narrative, short stories, poetry—or perhaps because questioning the historicity of the events is not as threatening for students when reading the Old Testament as when reading the New Testament, especially the Gospels. Kathleen O'Connor, a professor of Old Testament at Columbia Theological Seminary, says, "We expose the students to the historical-critical method, and I draw on it, but I'm really myself interested in literary approaches, looking at symbolic meanings, multiplicity of voices. Reader-response approaches feed what we do. We introduce dialogue between our context and the context of the ancient world."

One of the most common answers I heard, from students and faculty, in my own recent survey of methods taught for biblical study in theological education was reference to some form of what I would call "perspectivism." Several professors said that they commonly ask their students to read the text from the perspective of people of different identities, to read as a woman might, or an African American, or a person from a Latin American country, or as a gay or lesbian person. At some schools, this seems to be prompted or reinforced by the increasing diversity of the student body. As Ted Jennings from Chicago Theological Seminary noted, "Sometimes I do queer readings, or African American, or feminist. In a classroom we have students from all over: Asian, African American, women, queer, people from conservative backgrounds, and others who have barely seen a Bible. So in class discussions, issues come up that can be approached differently by the different students."

Indeed, especially at Chicago Theological Seminary (CTS), though at many other places as well, faculty and students both use certain words repeatedly to refer to such "perspectival" readings. At CTS, the most popular word I encountered was "lens." As Ken Stone put it, "Here, even in an introductory class, students have to look at the text through more than one lens." Laurel Schneider, who teaches theology at CTS, used the same word: "Even the nondoctoral students are aware that they are applying different lenses to the text, and that there is a variety. That becomes a crisis for a number of them: the Bible is not self-evident. And that relates to theology also, because they see that doctrines are not self-evident. Hermeneutics applies to theology and the production of theology. And the students who get that, and that it is a big part of the curricular expectation here, are the ones who really do well here." In this case, the responses I received from students at CTS suggest that the faculty were successful at least in teaching the notion that the text means different things when approached from different perspectives or through different "lenses."

In a very few schools, the emphasis on different perspectives for interpreting the Bible extends even to the teaching of more thorough reader-response criticism: the notion that texts have no meaning unless and until they are interpreted by actual readers, and that the meaning of the text will depend on how it is read. Ken Stone, for example, teaches several different methods, partly, he says, in order to teach them "how the reader helps create meaning." Many biblical scholars and students, however, hesitate to embrace reader-oriented approaches fully because they feel that to do so would necessarily lead to chaos or anarchy in interpretation or that people would willy-nilly read into the Scriptures simply what they want to see (the feared "eisegesis"). On the whole, more thorough reader-response criticism of the Bible, as well as "deconstructive" readings or even "allegorical" readings, find almost no place in most instruction in biblical studies in theological education, at least as far as I have been able to discern.

Some schools are doing more to de-emphasize the hegemony of historical criticism among different readings of Scripture or to teach it as only one approach among many. In particular, I noticed something of a difference, at least among the few schools I surveyed, between more "liberal" schools and those seeing themselves as "evangelical." The more "liberal" schools tended to teach other approaches in addition to historical criticism—though admittedly more likely feminist, literary, or perspectival approaches than thorough reader-response, deconstruction, or even allegory. At the more "evangelical" schools, students are taught mainly or only what I would call a historical-critical method: the meaning of the text is assumed to be the ancient author's intention or a range of understandings of an imagined ancient audience. Although concerns about eisegesis were voiced by students at almost every seminary or divinity school I visited, they were much more commonly expressed by students at evangelical seminaries, no doubt reflecting the self-image of such schools as communities that take the Bible (and only the Bible) to be the center of authority and the foundation for doctrine and ethics. Yet in spite of real differences among schools about how the Bible is authoritative, and thus different emphases on fears of eisegesis, the methods taught (basic grammatical-historical approaches) seem to be remarkably similar across the board in seminaries and divinity schools of widely varying theological slants.

In spite of attempts by some professors to introduce their students to a variety of ways of interpreting Scripture, therefore, the dominant method of interpretation students are taught, just about everywhere, is traditional historical criticism as described above. One student, who had already taken many courses in biblical studies at his seminary, said, "In terms of a 'method' it is mainly historical-critical. They introduce concepts of structuralism, post-structuralism, reader-response, for example, but their main approach is getting back to the author's intention, the original meaning of the text. In my experience, you might get a lecture introducing different methods, mainly to let you know 'what other people out there are doing.' But when they get down to it, it is mainly historical criticism." This statement came from a student who possessed a good bit of sophistication in interpretation theory, due actually to education in the subject he had gained as an undergraduate and in other courses. He was thus able to name with specific terms different interpretive possibilities and to identify the place of historical criticism among them.

Many students—even when they had taken several biblical studies courses—could not explicitly designate the historical-critical method itself. Yet it was clear upon further questioning that they were being taught mainly or exclusively historical-critical approaches. Furthermore, in most environments in which other approaches are introduced, it is done within the rubric of historical criticism (social-scientific approaches, for example, are introduced as an aid to understanding the ancient meaning of the text), or only as a secondary approach ancillary to a historical reading. Biblical studies professors and those teaching in other fields often noted that "historical criticism is a necessary starting point," or that even when other approaches are introduced, historical criticism "is the launching pad for whatever else they [the biblical faculty] do."

Some professors defend their preference for historical criticism on pedagogical or theological grounds. Historical criticism, they point out, enables students to "get some distance" on the text, to be able to look at the Bible with a new perspective, to help avoid a too-rapid "appropriation" of the text in ways that could be harmful or uncritical. Carol Newsom of Candler School of Theology, when asked what she thought of the historical-critical method, said, "It is a gift of the Holy Spirit because it allowed us to realize the distance between the text and ourselves, and it allows us, having recognized that distance, to enter the process of hermeneutical engagement with the text. . . . I tend to situate historical criticism within the theological enterprise." Julia O'Brien, at Lancaster Theological Seminary, said, "We have to understand that these texts have a history written in a particular context, politically, socially. We need to get that critical distance. The students need to know that the text didn't fall out of the sky written only for them. It might not have meant then what it means for you, and for me that is an ethical concern. You have to own up to your appropriation of it." Systematic theologian George Stroup, at Columbia Theological Seminary, similarly noted, "For all the problems many of us saw in the historical-critical method, the result now is that the students to some extent read the text ahistorically, and for some major ethical issues that can be devastating." And Margaret Aymer, at the Interdenominational Theological

Center, which teaches students from many different denominations and none, pointed out, "I'm trying to teach them some history, some literature, but also a lot of cultural criticism. [Much postmodern scholarship] is written for people steeped in historical criticism. I'm teaching people who are not. Some of them are at points in their lives where they are not even modernist, much less postmodernist. They are still in biblical inerrancy." In that kind of context, Aymer argued, critical historiography can be a first step in moving students toward a more sophisticated reading of the Bible.

Students often echo such sentiments. Donte Hilliard, a student at Chicago Theological Seminary, mentioned that he appreciated learning that the Hebrew Bible, understood historically, was first and foremost Jewish Scripture, and thinking of it that way had opened up for him new ways of seeing the text. "That's not a new concept to me, but I guess I hadn't thought to do that with Scripture. So I'm now excited about the Hebrew Bible in a way I've never been in my life, though I've been a Bible reader since I was, say, thirteen." Ed Dickel, a student at Lancaster, noted that teaching historical criticism within a context of different approaches helped teach students to read the text in a variety of ways. "They do teach historical criticism, but they do an excellent job of engaging our minds and helping us think critically about the text. There are important historical aspects, but they also point to current debate and things that might make our reading of the Bible change once again." In spite of some misgivings about historical criticism, and criticisms of its hegemony from some quarters, faculty and students both see that method as theologically and ethically useful: as a means of forcing Christians to look at the texts anew, a means of prying the text loose from the grip of a too-easy, self-serving, and possibly unethical appropriation.

BIBLICAL SCHOLARS AS "GATEKEEPERS"?

Most professors of Bible in theological schools, in my experience, see themselves as open-minded, theologically interested, and pedagogically innovative. They recognize their rootedness in modern (now rather traditional) historical-critical methods, but see themselves as introducing their students to other approaches as well. Moreover, the vast majority of them believe that they are teaching not only the historical meaning of the texts but also theological appropriations of Scripture, teaching how to move from a critical reading of the Bible to modern theological, ethical, and cultural application of its messages. One of the most interesting results of my own brief survey of seminaries and divinity schools was my discovery that the biblical faculty are seldom seen by their colleagues in other fields or by their students quite the same way.

First, the biblical faculty seldom speak of either the curriculum or the faculty as firmly divided by disciplinary boundaries. They usually see their own teaching as one part of a complex curriculum, and a part that easily interacts with other fields, such as theology, church history, ethics, preaching, and pastoral care. At one seminary, the biblical faculty expressed little concern about, or even knowledge of, disciplinary divisions or a lack of integration between biblical studies and other fields. Another professor at the same school, however, pointed to the lack of integration as particularly problematic for the students and the single aspect of the curriculum she would change if given the chance: "I would like to figure out how to integrate [biblical studies] intentionally. There is a big divide, and the students are having a hard time. How do you integrate the disciplines? That would be great." I encountered this sentiment regularly, but usually expressed by the nonbiblical faculty. The greatest division was felt to be not among all the different subject fields, but between the biblical faculty on the one side and all the other fields on the other.

The biblical curriculum and faculty are often seen by their colleagues as the most conservative methodologically. Even when the biblical professors see themselves as incorporating different approaches in their courses or stretching to teach theological interpretation, their colleagues regularly see them differently, in some cases as simply initiating their students into the older disciplinary knowledges and practices of modern biblical scholarship. One of the reasons for this, perhaps, is that biblical studies as a discipline, and perhaps New Testament studies even more so, tend to constitute methodologically a rather conservative discipline with a remarkable uniformity in the training of "professionals" for the field. Doctoral programs in New Testament studies around the country, for example, tend to be very similar to one another in their emphasis on philological and historical knowledge and techniques. It is perhaps no accident that scholars trained in such programs tend to teach those same approaches in the classroom. Thus, I regularly found, in traveling to different theological schools, that even in those places where the faculty are open to other approaches, the students are nonetheless still getting mostly historical criticism, as reflected in the answers students gave to survey questions. The dominance of historical criticism, or at least a strong emphasis on the ancient context and meaning of the text, may be to some extent a matter of disciplinary inertia within the field of biblical scholarship as a whole and the way it trains future seminary professors.

For example, even in a seminary in which the biblical faculty told me they were de-emphasizing historical criticism and teaching a wide variety of approaches to Scripture, faculty in adjacent fields perceived the situation otherwise, as these remarks illustrate:

> My impression is that [the biblical studies professors] do a great deal
> with the text as a historical text, that it has human authorship, history,
> things that can be traced. Stress is placed on understanding the texts
> in the context in which they were produced. For many students, the
> stress, for example, on reading the Hebrew Bible as Jewish texts first
> and foremost leaves them with the impression that reading them as
> Christian texts is inappropriate. I know that is not what [the biblical
> faculty] are trying to do, but I do sometimes hear that from students.

The professor then proceeded to bemoan the lack of integration of study of
Scripture with the other goals of the seminary: "Somehow I would like us all
to give our students a clearer sense of how we hear the voice of God in Scripture. That doesn't mean taking away the critical study. But I think the biblical
courses get focused too much on particular techniques and stresses that only
they provide. And somehow those don't get integrated into a wider sense of
how the church hears Scripture."

Another professor opined that the more sophisticated views of interpretation he knew the biblical faculty held were perhaps not reaching the students:

> Although they [the biblical faculty] are hermeneutically sophisticated,
> in what they actually teach they tend to do a lot of historical recon-
> struction of the original context and not much else. No deconstruc-
> tion, other literary readings, nothing like, for example, canonical style
> readings. . . . So students learn to do a lot of historical reconstruction
> of the original contexts, and then they get into history of theology and
> doctrine classes, and they can't see the connection. They're left won-
> dering, "How did Christians in the past use the Bible in such weird
> ways? Why were they so stupid as to do that?"

In the worst cases, professors of biblical studies are seen as gatekeepers in
the reading of the Bible, as exercising a censoring activity over the readings of
Scripture advanced by students and other professors, even when the biblical
faculty do not see themselves in that role. I have never met a professor, for
example, who claimed to teach "the only way" to read the Bible or who openly
aspired to monitor the use of the Bible throughout the seminary or curriculum. Yet in spite of this self-perception, biblical studies faculty are often seen
by their colleagues as assuming just such a gatekeeper role.

As one professor of theology put it, "In some of the other classes, students
are inclined to say, 'But you can't use the Bible that way.' If you are taught to
use the Bible differently in your pastoral care course than in the biblical studies courses, that sends a mixed message, and the students don't know what to
do with it. That comes through in their conversations and their preaching."
Another professor told about her early attempts to introduce students to readings of the Bible influenced by liberation theology: "The students were hav-

ing an anxiety attack because their exposure was through the historical-critical method, and the kinds of questions I was raising about the Bible were not those they had been taught in the Bible class. The students told me, 'You can't read the Bible like that.' One student in particular told me he had taken the exercise [I assigned] to his Bible professor, who told him, 'You can't read the Bible that way.'" Apparently, in spite of some of the best intentions of biblical scholars in theological schools, the perceptions of their students and their colleagues sometimes suggest that students are learning mainly historical-critical approaches to Scripture along with the notion that other meanings of the text may be inappropriate or at best secondary. In the worst cases, biblical scholars are actively playing roles as gatekeepers for biblical interpretation.

THEORY

Debates rage in our culture over interpretation of documents central to our culture, such as the Constitution and laws. Even in broader public debates in the "culture wars" over gender, sexuality, and the family, among other topics, interpretation of the Bible becomes an issue. This means that we must pay attention to how people interpret texts—not only for the sake of our churches, but also for the sake of our society. Critical attention to how people interpret texts is one of the central topics in literary theory, particularly in the subject we call "theory of interpretation." It is imperative that the leaders of our churches be trained to enter public debates with sophistication, equipped with the honed tools of contemporary interpretation theory.

In fact, all along, though without until now making it explicit, I have been talking about theory of interpretation, often in biblical studies called by its older, technical term, "hermeneutics." In my view, one of the great failures of contemporary theological education, especially with regard to the Bible, is the absence in almost all schools of the explicit education of students in interpretation theory.

"Theory" need not refer to anything highly rarified or complicated, though once people begin thinking critically about what actually happens when we interpret, complications usually do arise. At its most basic, interpretation theory is simply the explicit attempt to answer some basic questions. What is a text? People tend to work with some basic assumptions about texts. Is it like a box containing something we call "meaning"? Is it a puzzle we must figure out? Is it an opportunity for creating something, like the raw material for the production of meaning?

Is interpreting a text such as the Bible the same thing as interpreting the U.S. Constitution? Or an owner's manual for a car? Or is it more like interpreting a poem? Do we, should we, interpret all different kinds of texts in the same way? Or should we use different kinds of interpretive practices on different kinds of texts? That is, how is the accepted nature of the text (what kind of text it is) relevant for interpretation? Is interpreting a text the same thing as interpreting a painting? or abstract art? or music? or architecture? Do we, should we, allow ourselves more freedoms when interpreting nontextual artifacts than when interpreting texts? If so, why? If not, why not?

Can a text have more than one meaning? If so, is there a hierarchy of meanings, ranging from almost certainly correct, to legitimate, to allowable, to not acceptable? How are these decisions made, and by whom? Are allegorical interpretations legitimate? For example, is it legitimate to interpret the 1960s folk song "Puff the Magic Dragon" as an allegory for smoking marijuana? How about if the composer of the song insists that it was not written to be an allegory about smoking marijuana? In what contexts might an allegorical interpretation be okay? And why?

Is the anchor meaning of a text the author's intention? the ancient reader's likely understandings? or the readings of modern persons? What is the role of history (the history of the interpretation of the text) in interpreting ancient texts?

What is the relationship between textual interpretation and ethics? Are there simply unethical ways to treat a text? Are there unethical interpretations? If so, how do we discern those? If not, aren't we making textual interpretation irrelevant for much of our lives?

All such questions fall within the realm of interpretation theory, of hermeneutical theory. The teaching of interpretation theory, in my view, need not mandate steering students through a reading list of classics: say, Friedrich Schleiermacher, Hans Georg Gadamer, E. D. Hirsch, Ferdinand de Saussure, Michel Foucault, Jacques Derrida, Luce Irigaray, and Stanley Fish—though that is not a bad way to teach students to think critically about texts and interpretation. It need not include a fully rigorous immersion in philosophy, though again, philosophy has important things to teach us about the topic and its history. Interpretation theory may legitimately be taught in many different ways. But I believe students in most theological schools are not being taught how to think critically—that is, in a self-reflective way—about what it is they are doing, and should do, when they interpret texts. These are people who will be spending their lives interpreting texts, especially one central text for Christianity, and yet they do not know how to articulate with any sophistication what it is they are doing when they are doing it.

I should make it clear here, as I do in chapter 4 when speaking about theological interpretation in particular, that learning about theory of interpretation is not the same thing as learning to interpret. We all interpret texts all the time. Students in seminaries and divinity schools spend a huge amount of their time learning different practices and honing skills in actually interpreting texts. Interpretation *theory*, though, refers to second-order reflection on actual interpretation. It is the meta-level analysis of the primary-level activity of interpretation itself. It looks carefully and self-consciously at what people are doing, what we are doing when we read texts and other artifacts. It is also important, in my view indispensable, that students learn not only ways to interpret the Bible, but also how to think broadly and critically about the varied tasks of reading texts and using texts in society and the church. That is theory of interpretation.

Students are in fact imbibing in their schools certain assumptions about texts and meaning, certain implicit understandings of textuality and reading. These assumptions are simply not made explicit most of the time, and students are not taught to think about the assumptions in a critical way. Notice how different students at different schools talk about texts and meaning, even without realizing they are embodying a particular way of thinking about texts and meaning.

For example, when asked to describe how they are taught to interpret Scripture, students reveal different ideas about where "meaning" is located—in the text? in the author? in the past? in the reader?—even without being asked to address that issue. Students at Gordon-Conwell Theological Seminary said, "We're taught to lay aside our agendas and submit to the text." They said they are taught "exegesis, not eisegesis; what the text says." A student at Fuller Theological Seminary said that they were taught "a good open-mindedness to letting the text speak rather than pulling out these four verses that will back me up." Another said they were told to ask "not what it means for me, but for the author and the people he wrote to." A student at North Park Seminary said that the focus was "not reading into the text, eisegesis, but trying to discover what the text is saying in its context of history." According to these students, the text is something that contains meaning or speaks its own message. The primarily correct meaning is related to the ancient context of the text.

Students at most of the other schools I visited also emphasized the historical meaning as providing at least the first meaning or the starting point of interpretation. But they added that they were sometimes introduced to other ways of reading the text that were not limited to historical criticism. As mentioned above, they sometimes spoke of these other readings as different "perspectives" on the text. A student at the University of Chicago Divinity School, for instance, said, "We are taught to speak of ourselves as interpreters and adopt a point of view, such as feminist, liberation theology, or reader-response." Students at these other schools spoke of some introduction of reader-response approaches, or feminist readings, or postcolonial approaches. In almost all cases, though, the students mentioned these different approaches as supplementing historical criticism, and as secondary to it. Of the ten schools I visited, only at Chicago Theological Seminary did I encounter students who spoke about the historical method as only one among many different methods of interpretation, and on an equal level with the other methods. They were taught to read Scripture through "the lens of your own experience, and other lenses than your own," naming in particular feminist, African American, queer, womanist, and Latin American lenses.

This brief survey suggests, therefore, that students do actually imbibe, even without realizing it, different assumptions about what texts are and how they should be interpreted. Some assume that the location of "meaning" is basically in the past, in the author's intention or the ancient context, now vouchsafed to them in the container of the text, which their professors will teach them to open. Others assume that the full meaning of the text is experienced only in the particular reading experiences of modern persons. Others seem to embrace the assumption that meaning is itself multiple and ever-expanding. The problem is that students often do not realize that they are actually working with these assumptions. I am arguing that they should be educated to analyze such assumptions critically, which means teaching them to think theoretically about interpreting texts.

Professors give various answers when asked about the teaching of interpretation theory in their courses or school. Some point out that resources do exist in their institutions where students can study hermeneutics and philosophical theories of interpretation, but they admit that students can easily avoid exposure to such courses and discussions. Some bemoan the lack of more attention to interpretation theory. Others respond, rather naively in my view, that they are not interested in teaching method or theory; they are just interested in teaching the students "basic reading and writing," "to respond to the texts appropriately." It seems to go unnoticed by such professors that they actually are teaching the students at least one method if they are teaching them anything at all about how to read and write. One cannot teach students to read without implicitly teaching them a method of reading. In some cases, faculty believe they are teaching hermeneutical theory, but I often suspected that they were doing so more by implication than explicitly. In at least some cases, even faculty who worked with rather sophisticated notions of the complexities of interpretation, including theoretical scholarship on the topic, clearly were not making those subjects part of their courses in biblical studies.

In my experience, students usually do not understand basic questions of a theoretical nature. They often seem puzzled when asked about what methods they are taught for reading the Bible. Not only do they usually not know what the term "interpretation theory" or "hermeneutics" means, but even when those terms are unpacked for them, they do not know even how to think about questions such as "what is a text?" or any of a number of the questions posed above.

The problem is that many Bible instructors believe that they are teaching students to think theoretically simply by introducing them to different interpretive options. As one professor who teaches in a different field put it, "Some faculty think that's built into the way the Bible is taught, but they are confusing teaching plurality of interpretation with teaching theory. Many of the smarter students recognize the plurality, but if you ask them to articulate their theory, they haven't been given the tools to do that." Education in interpretation theory goes beyond introducing students simply to different practices of interpretation. Students will be taught a particular method or several methods of reading, which will include assumptions about the nature of texts, meaning, and correct or incorrect practices of interpretation. Students should therefore learn to think critically about these issues. That is what "theory" in interpretation is. Unfortunately, judging from my experiences and observations, theological students seldom receive adequate training in interpretation theories.

THEOLOGICAL INTERPRETATION

A similar situation prevails with regard to theological interpretation. As is the case with teaching theory of interpretation, teaching theological interpretation, or theological hermeneutics, need not refer to anything particularly daunting or specific. "Theological interpretation" means simply interpreting the text of the Bible *as Scripture*, the "word of God." Of course, this should entail some discussion of what it means to call a text "Scripture." What do we mean by "the word of God"? But anyone should be able to recognize that taking the Bible to be nothing more than a historical artifact will produce different readings of it than if one takes it to be divine communication, whatever that may mean. Exploring that difference is the fundamental activity of theology of interpretation, which is itself necessary for an informed and self-aware theological interpretation.

Theology of interpretation—and thus theological interpretation as different from, say, purely historical or literary interpretation—raises important questions for Christians. What is the nature of Scripture? Should we understand it as a rule book? a constitution? a foundational document? a "space" we occupy? What does it mean to say that Scripture is "inspired"? What are different models for understanding the function of Scripture for the church? As an "authority"? And what do we mean by "authority"? Does the concept of "authority" introduce issues of domination and hierarchy that may no longer be appropriate in a church that has accepted more egalitarian ideas of society and justice?

How are our notions of Scripture and its interpretation related to our beliefs and confessions about the Holy Spirit? What do we really believe the

Holy Spirit does in our lives and communities? How does the Holy Spirit relate to our readings of Scripture? How do we conceive of the role of the Holy Spirit in individual and communal interpretations of Scripture?

Do our beliefs about Scripture relate to our beliefs about incarnation? Is the "word of God" embodied in the text related to the "word of God" embodied in Jesus Christ? If so, how? Why do we use the phrase "word of God" for both Scripture and Jesus?

What are the proper methods to be used by Christians when reading the Bible as Scripture? Is historical criticism necessary? If so, why? If not, why not? Allegorical interpretations of Scripture have been used throughout the history of Christianity, especially until the rise of modernity. Are allegorical readings of Scripture still proper for us? If not, why not? May we, in our interpretations of the Old Testament, the Hebrew Bible, use the same freedoms of interpreting the text we see practiced by Jesus in the Gospels? by Paul in his letters? by the author of Hebrews? If not, why not? If so, may that lead to chaos of interpretation and eisegesis?

The different questions raised by issues of theological hermeneutics are many and could be multiplied ad infinitum. But they all basically come down to central issues concerning the nature of Scripture and how it should be interpreted in the life of the church and in the lives of individual Christians. This sort of training is being neglected in much contemporary theological education. Students are in fact interpreting the Bible theologically, but they are seldom taught to think about how they do or could or should interpret the Bible theologically. Again, they are not taught to think critically and in a self-aware manner about theological interpretation even while they are interpreting theologically. This situation leads, in my view, sometimes simply to unimaginative theological applications of Scripture—and therefore often to dull sermons—but in worse cases to theologically or ethically dangerous interpretations of Scripture.

By far the majority of biblical scholars teaching in theological schools believe they are introducing their students to theological hermeneutics. Admittedly, a few seem to avoid the issue, at least to some extent, because they assume that theological interpretation will in and of itself be too univocal. One professor, for instance, when asked about whether he teaches theological hermeneutics, said, "We don't do the 'meta' issues in my approach. I'm more interested in [the students] raising questions and engaging the diversity. I don't want to impose [theological interpretation] too early." Another said she was concerned about allowing theological approaches to delimit diversity of meaning: "I'm somewhat wary of some theological readings because students still take it as authoritative if it is bound in a book. Some of them take it as gospel truth, and I'm trying to get them to see that there are many gospel truths."

These responses assume that theological interpretation will of necessity be only a unitary interpretation or will close off diversity. Another professor seemed to believe that students would get guidance in theological interpretation from their own denominations: "Their own traditions will have ways of [dealing with the] authority of the Bible," therefore absolving him of the need to address such issues. It is not at all clear, however, that this is the case.

In spite of these few voices to the contrary, most biblical scholars claim that their students are being taught theological interpretation "constantly," in "all" their classes. What they mean by this is that students are regularly being asked questions such as, "So what might this passage mean for us today? How would you preach from this passage in your church?" It is not clear, though, that being told simply to "apply" the text theologically is the same as teaching students critical tools for learning how to do so or for reflecting on what it means to do so. And though most professors are doing the former, very few even attempt the latter. As one professor said, "There is a sense in which all these things overlap. So doing history is part of doing theology. I've never in my imagination or teaching separated theology from history or anthropology as if they are discrete disciplines in the end. I never say, 'Now we're going to do theology' rather than something else. I don't extricate it. But the 'meta' level of reflection on reading theologically? I think a lot of that is picked up inductively, and I assume they are getting some of that in the theology courses."

In my experience, though, both at the school of that professor as well as many others, students are not learning inductively to think critically about what theological interpretation is, nor are they usually taught it in theology courses. As a theology professor elsewhere put it, "Teaching application of the Bible is not teaching theological hermeneutics. We don't have a place in the curriculum where students are forced to think clearly about how they want to think about interpreting the Bible with theology." Note the phrasing: "forced to think clearly about how they want to think." That secondary reflection on the practice of how Christians should interpret theologically, not simply using the text for theological ends, constitutes theological hermeneutics.

The responses of students regularly suggest that here too, as was the case with theory of interpretation, they are not getting it. When asked if they are taught "theological interpretation" of the Bible, students regularly respond with something like (these being the actual words of one student), "Theological interpretation? I'm not sure what you are asking." Students who did understand the question usually responded negatively, as in this example: "Theological hermeneutics? Not in any extensive way. We're definitely not called on to try different hermeneutics. Different professors will talk about theological issues, and so we kind of pick up different ideas. But it isn't named, in the sense that 'This is what inspiration means,' or 'What does it mean for

this to be Scripture?' or 'Is the canon closed?' and all that." Another student,
who had learned about hermeneutics as an undergraduate, noted that theological hermeneutics at his seminary was "implicit" but perhaps should be
addressed more explicitly: "I think a couple of days at the beginning on theories of reading and theologies of interpretation [should be taught]. There are
still people in my classes at the end of the second year giving simplistic
homiletical readings. This isn't a weakness of the professors, but sometimes
students remain in a Sunday school world." This student recognized, because
of exposure to interpretation theory elsewhere, that his own institution was
not doing a very good job of providing students with the critical skills in thinking theologically about Scripture and the theological interpretation of Scripture. In seminaries and divinity schools, students who will spend their careers
being called upon to interpret the Bible for theological and ethical ends are
not being sufficiently trained in how to think and speak articulately about
theological interpretation.

INTEGRATION

During the twentieth century the typical curriculum of a theological education, especially in "mainline" Protestant seminaries and divinity schools
though elsewhere as well, became increasingly divided into different specialties or areas of study, which may be thought of as different disciplines on the
model of the different areas of research in a modern university.[4] In a modern
theological school, some instructors specialize in teaching systematic theology, others in church history, others in pastoral counseling, or preaching, or
Christian education, to name a few. In the nineteenth century, scholars began
specializing in biblical studies, and increasingly in the twentieth century in
either Old Testament (Hebrew Bible) or New Testament. Nowadays in the
United States, biblical scholars or church historians do not usually call themselves "theologians," unless they also specialize to some extent in the study and
teaching of systematic or applied theology, and the entire faculty is not called
"the faculty of theology." (The case is different in many countries in Europe,
where the term "theology" often covers all those teaching any subject related
to the study of Christianity.) In the United States those designations are generally reserved for faculty teaching specifically systematic, historical, or
applied theology. This issue of nomenclature reflects the development of academic specialization in theological education during the twentieth century.

Over the course of the twentieth century, in the various fields of study that
may be thought of as different disciplines, the research and teaching of seminary subjects became in most places grouped into four separate curricular areas,

commonly referred to by historians of the topic as "the fourfold curriculum." One area comprised biblical studies, both Old and New Testaments. Another comprised theological studies proper, including systematic, dogmatic, and philosophical theology, often including history of theology, and maybe philosophy of religion and ethics. A third area was church history, from the late ancient church (patristics), through the history of Christianity in Europe, and into the history of religion in America. The fourth came to be a clustering of all those subjects or practices deemed "practical" training for the pastor or church worker: homiletics or preaching, pastoral care and counseling, Christian education, and in some places including subjects such as liturgics, missiology, or, increasingly, spiritual formation. Indeed, what subjects were grouped within the fourth area varied substantially according to the particular denominational needs, the particular strengths of the school, and the different fashions of the time. This fourth area of practical theology or practical ministerial skills in some schools resembles a grab bag of whatever is left over after establishing the more classical areas of biblical studies, theology, and church history. The history of this curricular development is an interesting story in itself, as other studies have emphasized. For my purposes, it is sufficient to note its growing dominance throughout the twentieth century in theological education.[5]

The organization of courses and faculty in some schools follows this fourfold curriculum faithfully. For example, at Princeton Theological Seminary, the faculty are assigned to one of four primary departments, listed on the Web site as (1) biblical studies, (2) theology, (3) history, and (4) practical theology. The curricula of other schools reflect the now traditional fourfold curriculum but with some differences. Candler School of Theology at Emory University, though in the process of revising its curriculum, currently lists its four areas as (1) biblical studies, (2) history and interpretation of Christianity (which includes theology), (3) Christianity and culture (sociology, ethics, world religions, among others), and (4) practical ministry. Others retain the classical four with some additions. North Park Theological Seminary lists its areas as (1) biblical, (2) historical, (3) theological, and (4) ministerial, and then adds (5) spiritual formation. Some schools arrange all subjects into three rather than four areas. Chicago Theological Seminary lists its areas as (1) Christian heritage (including history of Christian thought and biblical studies), (2) theology, ethics, and contemporary culture, and (3) Christian ministries. Master of divinity students at the University of Chicago Divinity School are required to take courses in three different areas, listed as (1) historical studies (including Bible), (2) constructive studies (including theology and ethics), and (3) religion and human sciences.

My use of lists here, including even numerals, is intended to highlight a few points. First, the schools themselves typically present the divisions of their

faculty and curricula in just such a hierarchical manner. Second, biblical studies are often in a category alone, more often, in fact, than any other "discipline," though in some cases biblical studies are combined with historical
studies more generally. Third, it is also significant that biblical studies are
almost always listed as the first field, as area number one. This hierarchical
arrangement is not one of my own making, but reflects the presentations of
the schools themselves.

The hierarchy of the different subject areas is not a matter of mere public rep-
resentation. In conversations with students and even sometimes faculty, the field
of biblical studies is either perceived or considered to perceive itself as the most
foundational of the different subject areas—sometimes as the most scientific or
rigorous of the subjects. This is matched by the fact that when seminaries and
divinity schools attempt to sequence the courses students take—to have students
take certain courses or subjects in a particular order—they most often require
or encourage students to begin their theological education with courses in biblical studies. With modifications here and there, the divisions and the hierarchy
of the fourfold curriculum manifest themselves in the faculty organizations and
curricula of most seminaries and divinity schools in the United States.

The disciplinary development of subjects in religious studies and theology
has had great benefits for the study of religion in the world, perhaps especially
in the United States. The extent and level of scholarship in biblical studies,
theology, ethics, church history, and all the other fields are perhaps at an all-
time high. Excellent and well-published scholars occupy the classrooms of
large and small divinity schools and seminaries throughout the country. The
sheer number of significant books and articles published and papers presented
at scholarly conferences is staggering. Most of us find that we cannot even keep
up with important publications in our own area of specialization, such as New
Testament studies, or Hebrew Bible, or systematic theology, or church history—to say nothing of "the study of Christianity" or other religious traditions. The growth in the abundance and sophistication of scholarship on
subjects in religion would not have been possible without the growth in specialization of scholarship. The division of the general study of theology into
different fields or disciplines has therefore had a salutary effect on the scholarly study of religion throughout the world, including North America.

Those benefits, however, have been offset by the problems such division
and specialization generate for students who too often must themselves integrate what they are learning in different areas of the curriculum. Those problems are perhaps most difficult, if one is to believe what students themselves
say, in their attempts to integrate what they are learning in courses on the Bible
with the other subjects, especially theology and ethics. As one student put it,
"By the time you are done with some of these classes, you forget how to read

the Bible through the lens of faith, of a tradition. Coming at it academically is refreshing but also exhausting because it rubs differently. It is a mixed blessing. It is valuable to be able to read the texts historical-critically. Conversely, I think it retards the development of a theological interpretation of the text. I don't think that is nurtured."

This is not to imply that professors themselves do not recognize the problem. Administrators and faculty regularly express concerns about disciplinary overspecialization and division, and many of them struggle to figure out ways to help students integrate different knowledges and skills they are being taught in different courses. Donald Hagner at Fuller, for instance, confessed, "I'm afraid my perception is that we are in airtight compartments, even between Old Testament and New Testament. . . . But I think it is a symptom of over-specialization. It is not, to my knowledge, being done deliberately." Problems of integration in theological education seem to have been chronic since the development of modern scholarly specialization and the formation of seminary curricula in imitation of such concentrations. In spite of the best intentions of faculty and administrators, problems of integration—especially between biblical studies and theology—persist.

CONCLUSION

Though much of this chapter is based on my own perceptions and limited observations, supplemented by a few more extensive studies by others, it may be taken, I believe, to be at least one fair perspective on the role of biblical studies in contemporary theological education. I think further research would likely support my basic points:

1. Historical criticism (as defined and described above) of one type or another is dominant as *a* or even *the* foundational method taught to most theological students for interpreting Scripture, in all sorts of schools of different theological leanings and denominational or nondenominational affiliation.
2. Most students are not being taught to think critically about textuality and interpretation in general. They are not being taught interpretation theory at any sophisticated level, with the result that they express naïve notions about interpretation and textual meaning. The lack of theoretical skill in imagining how interpretation does and may take place puts limits on their own abilities to interpret the Bible in creative and imaginative ways.
3. Students are not being taught theological hermeneutics sufficiently, meaning that they will be less likely to function as well-equipped guides for teaching responsible and creative theological interpretation of the Bible to members of their own religious communities.

4. Although biblical illiteracy is a problem in our culture, and thus also a problem for our theology students, the main problem is not merely a lack of biblical knowledge but a lack of ability to think theologically—that is, the ability to put together a theological argument, case, or rationale. The move from reading Scripture to making appropriate Christian use of Scripture is impeded by a basic lack of theological skill or know-how.
5. Students are not being helped enough to integrate the different disciplines learned in a typical ministerial education, with the main problematic division being between biblical studies and all the other areas.
6. The modern theological school, in far too many cases, is not doing a good job of teaching church leaders to interpret the Bible in creative, imaginative, and theologically sophisticated ways.

The following chapters address these different theses and attempt some suggestions for further thought.

2

Readers and Texts

"It is exegesis, and they've warned us about doing eisegesis. Exegesis is pulling out the meaning that is really there, and eisegesis is trying to impart a meaning to the text that I want it to have to fit some motive, or by accident, or by poor scholarship."

"They try to keep us tightly connected into the Bible: what's the basis for this biblically, not how people have taken the verses out of context and preached them, but what they're saying themselves."

"I can't say there was a particular method taught [in my Bible courses]. It was important to read the text and take it for what it is."

"Being true to what the text holds."

Student comments such as these make it clear that one of the central ideas students are taught about interpretation is a supposed difference between exegesis and eisegesis, as I mentioned in the previous chapter. In some situations, the two terms may be useful. Teaching students to hold off on asking what the text has to say to them personally today, or theologically to the contemporary church, can sometimes be a good thing. It does help students gain some critical distance on the Bible by emphasizing what its historical meaning may have been before rushing too quickly to a devotional use or contemporary interpretation or modern ethical application. But I am convinced that the emphasis on the difference between exegesis and eisegesis currently does more harm than good in teaching students about biblical interpretation. It reinforces a notion about texts and meaning that is false in itself, as this chapter argues. It

29

reinforces the commonsensical but mistaken idea that texts simply have mean-ing as a property within themselves, that texts dispense their meaning them-selves, or that texts may constrain interpretations of themselves.

Students, usually encouraged by their professors but often simply reflect-ing a common sense of our society, work with certain images about texts and meaning. They use particular metaphors when talking about textual interpre-tation. One such image pictures texts as containers, like boxes, that hold mean-ing inside them. Learning to interpret the Bible in seminary is pictured as learning how to open the box, unpack and perhaps discard the rather useless packing materials, and pull the meaning out of the text. In this image of inter-pretation, the student is active, but only by getting through layers of textual-ity (the box and packing) in order to find the meaning. The meaning, in any case, is objectively there, simply hidden in the container of the text.

Another image treats the text as if it were another human agent who speaks. In this case, the meaning is the utterance of the text. The job of the student is to be as passive as possible, listen as carefully and objectively as possible, and try to avoid distorting the utterance. In this image, the student is even more passive than in the box image: the interpretation process is a matter of just listening.

The problem with these images of texts and meaning is that they are metaphors that become accepted as realities. Texts are not just containers that hold meaning. The meaning of a text is a result of the interpretive process itself, which is not possible apart from the activities of human interpreters. And texts are not agents who speak. No text has ever spoken. What people mean when they talk that way about texts is that they, the human interpreters, have imag-ined their own reading practices as if they were listening to a voice coming from the text or from the author imagined to stand behind the text. But these metaphors give people the false impression that texts can control their own interpretation. If we believe someone else is "misreading" a text, we can take the person back to that text, ask the text again what it is "saying," and demonstrate to that person by the text's own agency that his or her interpretation is incorrect and ours is better. Contrary to this common misconception, however, if we are in fact successful in changing another person's mind about the text's meaning, it will have been our agency that affected our friend's reading of the text, not any fictitious agency of the text itself. Texts cannot dispense their meaning, and they cannot control their interpretation. Those activities are done by human beings.

The problem with language about exegesis versus eisegesis is that it implies that the difference between the two exists in objective reality or that it is embodied in particular methods of interpretation. Neither assumption is cor-rect. After all, my exegesis is usually someone else's eisegesis and vice versa. Almost no one thinks that she or he is reading into the text a meaning that is not really there. All readings of texts in fact are the making of meaning. So all language about "listening" to a text, or "hearing it," or "taking it on its own terms" employ metaphors that mask what is actually happening: interpretation practiced by human agents. Thus one of my favorite slogans: Texts don't mean; people mean with texts.[1]

READERS OF TEXTS

My statements here about texts and meaning are still controversial in some quarters, though less among scholars of literature or literary theory, perhaps most of whom nowadays assume that of course texts must be interpreted before they can be meaningful to human beings. Biblical scholars have been slower to give up the fiction that texts may control their own interpretation and dispense their own meaning. Since the 1980s, however, the fiction has been increasingly difficult to sustain.

In the 1970s and 1980s, the writings of certain literary theorists and professors of English became famous for arguing that texts do not themselves contain or create meaning. Briefly put, these literary critics argued—mainly from rather simple empirical observation of how human beings do in fact get meaning from spots on a page we call "texts"—that textual meaning is something created by human beings practicing rather complicated socially learned skills we call "reading." The most famous advocate of these ideas was Stanley Fish. To illustrate his point, Fish recalled a little experiment he had conducted with some of his students who were taking a course with him on interpreting symbolic poetry. As Fish explains, "These students had been learning how to identify Christian symbols and how to recognize typological patterns and how to move from the observation of these symbols and patterns to the specification of a poetic intention that was usually didactic or homiletic."[2] During a previous class in the same room, Fish had written on the chalkboard a list of names of authors he had been discussing while teaching on a completely different topic. The names were arranged on the board like this:

Jacobs-Rosenbaum
Levin
Thorne
Hayes
Ohman (?)

Fish notes that he had originally placed the question mark in parentheses after the last name because he couldn't remember whether it was spelled with one "n" or two. Before the next group of students entered the room, Fish simply drew a frame around the names and wrote "p. 43" on top of the frame.

Once the students were settled in the classroom, Fish told them this was a poem and asked them to intepret it, which they proceeded to do with no hesitation. One student pointed to the spatial arrangement of the words and suggested it could invoke a cross or an altar. Another interpreted "Jacob" by reference to Jacob's ladder. We could imagine them interpreting "Thorne" as a reference to a crown of thorns, and "Rosenbaum" also as a religious symbol ("rose-tree"). Because the students had been taught how to interpret religious, symbolic poems and had been told this text was precisely that, they had no trouble making perfect sense out of the text, even though the text had originally been a mere list of authors. The students needed no actual "author's intention" (though they clearly could have assumed an author's intention of their own imagination). Obviously the meaning of the poem was not simply a property contained by the text in the normal, commonsense way of thinking of such. As Fish concludes, "As soon as my students were aware that it was poetry they were seeing, they began to look with poetry-seeing eyes, that is, with eyes that saw everything in relation to the properties they knew poems to possess."[3]

Another famous example of this sort of experiment comes courtesy of Jonathan Culler. First, Culler offers what he intentionally composed to be a "nonsense" string of words, arranged, nonetheless, to reflect correct English syntax: "Colourless green ideas sleep furiously." Next, Culler spends pages demonstrating that a reader can make very good sense out of the sentence, such as this, admittedly rather silly-sounding, interpretation: "Bland and as yet unripe ideas, or perhaps ideas of a 'greening' of the world, lead a life of furious dormancy, repressed because of their blandness and able to accede to their potential fury only if they are awoken by an imaginative infusion of life and colour."[4] Regardless of what we may think of Culler's own making sense of his initially nonsense statement, it does demonstrate an important fact about all readings of texts: readers make sense of texts; texts do not dispense their meaning, nor is meaning dependent on authorial intention.

I want to be clear that I am here referring not to a particular method of reading or interpreting texts, one method that may be utilized among others. Rather I am talking about an account of making meaning in general, about how texts actually do come to mean something for people, about how human beings in fact interpret texts. I am not talking about one way of reading texts among others, but about how reading does in fact happen. One can, of course, make use of reader-response methods for interpretation. When the professors at Chicago Theological Seminary, for instance, urge their students to put on different lenses for reading Scripture, they are invoking these ideas as a method for reading, as one approach for interpreting the text among others. They teach the students that the text may have one meaning when read by an African American and another when read by a white, gay or lesbian Christian, that it may have one meaning when read in a Latin American base community and another when read by a middle-class feminist theologian. They are showing that each of these may be legitimate readings that could exist alongside the historical-critical reading of the text. This is to treat reader-response as one method of reading among others, and it is a legitimate and fine appropriation of these ideas.

But I am here speaking of something rather different. I am here providing an account of how texts in general come to have meaning for human beings at all, for how human beings all get meaning from a text, or more accurately, make meaning with texts. I am not saying that this is the way we ought to read texts. Nor am I saying that this is the way human beings make meaning because it feels that way. In fact, the notion that readers make meaning actually feels counterintuitive to most of us because we so readily feel that texts give us their meaning or contain meaning. Nonetheless, I insist that this is a description of human interpretation based on observation of how human beings in different contexts and with different texts actually do interpret texts. In other words, I am here relating an empirical account of human interpretation and textual meaning.

By "empiricism" I don't mean anything particularly philosophical, much less a notion that there is a simple, objective reflection of reality. I simply mean that if we analyze what happens when people interpret texts, we can see that the texts themselves are not really agents that control their interpretation or dispense their meaning, but that human beings make meaning in different ways when they read texts, even when they read the same texts. The evidence supporting this observation is constituted by fairly simple, everyday examples of how language functions in human society.

Even examples given by scholars who oppose this argument—examples they offer to disprove its account of textual meaning—actually support my argument. Richard Hays, for example, attempts to dismiss the entire idea with one simple example: he says that we all know perfectly well what the letters "STOP" mean when we see them on a stop sign.[5] Of course, if I am driving a motorized vehicle and come to such a sign, read the letters, and stop my vehicle, I do show that I take the text to mean, "This is a command to stop your vehicle here, look for other traffic, and proceed only when you have the right-of-way as defined by local traffic laws." In that case, that is the meaning of the text. But what if a high school boy shows up in the middle of the night, steals the sign, and hangs it up in his bedroom? If I see the sign in his bedroom, should I still think that there it also means that I am supposed to stop my vehicle at the foot of his bed? Or let's say that the sign is hung on the wall of the Museum of Modern Art. Does "STOP" have the same meaning there? Of course not. The meaning of the letters and the sign all shift according to where it is presented and how. As a competent user of English and a competent interpreter of signs I must be able to interpret the text to mean something different when I encounter it in different contexts. The text "STOP" doesn't contain its meaning in itself, nor is its meaning located in some author's intention. Its meaning is a social product produced by competent interpreters of a given culture.

One situation that demonstrates the complexities of normal, everyday interpretation is the use of a language by persons who are not yet completely competent speakers of the language. When I was at the beginning stages of learning Spanish and traveling from my home in Texas to a new home in Guatemala, I tried to order breakfast in a Mexican diner. I asked the waiter, "Tiene huevos?" My intention was to ask, "Do you have eggs?" which is certainly a literal translation of those two Spanish words. But in this case, it was not the meaning of my statement. At the time, I was puzzled that the waiter first scowled at me, and then grinned. I found out later that I had actually asked the young man, "Do you have balls?" (of the testicular, not soccer, type). Note that the meaning of the question in this case could not be identified with either my intention or some property contained in the text. The correct interpretation would be the product of the exercise of several different aspects of cultural knowledge, aspects that any human being would have to learn from society more generally. To understand even my own question correctly (that is, in ways that native speakers would accept as a right interpretation), I needed more socialization in the linguistic conventions of the culture.

With more complex linguistic phenomena the interpretive process may itself become more complicated, but at base it is still the same process. A phone book, for instance, may be read to derive information for calling other people on the phone. In that case, the meaning of the text is quite correctly taken to be the delivery of practical information. But a creative literature professor might very well use a phone book to teach students how to read and write poetry. The professor might, for example, ask the students to treat every other name as a verb, take the numbers to refer to letters of the alphabet, and contrive strings of words that create a new meaning from the old pieces of data. Have the students misread the text of the phone book? Only if we insist that the only legitimate use of a phone book is to deliver practical information. But why should we do that?

Processes of reading and making meaning are not, of course, limited to those objects we normally call "texts." The way we interpret art, for example, follows the same basic procedures. The meaning of a piece of art cannot be limited to some kind of meaning intended by the artist, nor does the piece contain its meaning simply within itself. In many museums and galleries one may encounter found art: a tire, a rope, a newspaper, or a pile of rocks is placed on the floor of a museum and suddenly becomes not just a piece of trash but now a piece of art. What makes the object now art? It is not some property in the object, but the social context and a tacit social agreement that we will treat the object as art. And museumgoers need not worry about what the artist intended the piece to mean, though of course they may well wonder about that. In any case, the meaning of the art object—the tire, rope, whatever—will be the result of interpretation performed by some human being who has been socialized to "read" art in a museum.

SOME COMMON COUNTERARGUMENTS

Although these ideas of texts and readers have become generally accepted in scholarly circles—to the extent that they are basically now common sense in many places—biblical scholars have often resisted them. A few have offered explicit objections or counterarguments. One of the most common is the observation that we all feel when we read that we are not ourselves creating meaning but are hearing, seeing, or getting meaning from the text. People will say, "But I didn't make the meaning I saw in the text; in fact, I was thinking something entirely different, and the text changed my mind." The feeling we readers have that we are ourselves changed by texts provides some people with sufficient evidence that texts give out their meaning.

But again, let's actually observe the reading activity. When I look at spots on a page—a text—I am of course looking at something, and the spots on this page may not be the same as the spots on another page. I am not making meaning out of nothing. I am reacting to something that is really there. But the problem with many people's assumptions when they oppose the self to the text as two different entities is that they assume that the self is a stable thing and that in order to be changed it must be changed by some other agent that can dispense meaning. But the self is no such stable entity.

When I left my house this morning I noticed that the sky was an unusually clear, crisp blue, that the clouds looked like bunnies, and that the day felt especially cheery. This put me in a good mood, and I began thinking about taking my dog for a hike. Notice that in this scenario, meaning has taken place. My very self was changed, even if slightly, by my interaction with the weather and the outdoors. In my looking at the sky and the clouds and feeling the air I became altered a bit, and the idea came to me that it would be a good day for a hike with my dog. Did the weather communicate that to me? Did it give me the idea to go for a walk? Did the sky, like an agent, convince me to be cheerful? We could of course talk that way metaphorically, but we would be just confused if we actually believed that all that meaning was just sitting there in the sky and clouds communicating cheeriness and hikes to me.

In fact, my own mind created all that meaning by reacting to the stimuli of the weather and my environment. In the same way, there certainly are marks on the page, but my mind is necessary for those marks to become meaningful for me. I may feel as if there is another thing, voice, or mind communicating to me through or from those marks, but that feeling is my projection of an inner dialogue that is going on in my mind. I think dialogically and then project one of those voices outside myself onto the text. Then that very process of reaction, that process of interpreting, itself causes a change, even if slightly, in my self. Our selves are constantly changing, and so the process of reading and interpreting a text will also change us. But it is not the inanimate text that is the agent of change; the process of interpretation we ourselves are practicing changes us.

This explanation also clarifies confusion some people introduce when they object that if I am correct, we all simply look into texts and see ourselves reflected back at us. Reading in that case would always be solipsistic. This assumes, though, that the self is more stable than it is. The self is constantly being altered by all aspects of our environment. If I read the same text tomorrow as I read today, I will probably have at least a slightly different experience of the text, not because the text itself has changed, but because my self has changed. The fear of solipsism in reading exaggerates the stability of the human self. The fact that selves change means that no two encounters with a text will be entirely the same: it is not exactly the same "self" that reads the text at different times.

Some people grab onto difference itself to argue that texts contain their meaning. Since the spots on the page *are* different from those on another page, and since I interpret one set of spots differently than I do another set of spots, doesn't that demonstrate that the spots have meaning in themselves? Not really. I interpret the spots in the ways I do because I have been taught to do so in certain ways. I have been socialized to make a certain kind of sense out of a set of spots arranged one way, and another kind of sense out of spots arranged a different way. But if I had not had that socialization—if I had not been taught to read and to read in particular ways—the spots would have no meaning for me, which also explains why another common counterargument is false. Some people will say, "But if readers are the ones creating meaning with the text, how do you explain that many different readers will 'see' the same meaning in the same text?" The answer is obvious: because they have been socialized in the same or similar ways to make meaning of texts of the same sort. Different human beings read texts the same way to the extent—and only to the extent—that they have been commonly socialized to read.

Some scholars have made this point by talking about communities of readers, reading communities, or interpretive communities.[6] Others prefer to talk about "sets" of skills we have learned to use in reading or "reading formations"—in A. K. M. Adam's words, "various conflicting economic and social constraints that compete for the reader's allegiance."[7] No human being comes at texts as a blank or in complete isolation from other human beings. Even when we are alone, we carry around in our heads our reading community (or more precisely, communities, since we are not influenced by only one set of reading assumptions but by several). We have learned proper and improper ways to read texts, and we have learned that different kinds of texts should be interpreted with different kinds of practices. So we don't read a stop sign the same way while driving as when we see it in a museum. We don't usually read a phone book as if it were poetry. We don't read poetry as if it were an owner's manual for our car. But in all these cases, the text is not telling us the proper way to read it; we ourselves are putting into practice reading strategies and assumptions we have internalized, practices that have become so second nature to us that we don't even reflect on how we are in fact reading and making meaning. All human beings are socialized into ways of reading, and insofar as people are commonly socialized, they will tend to read the same texts in the same ways.

This explanation provides the answer to the "Humpty-Dumpty" objection. Some scholars enjoy quoting the scene from *Through the Looking Glass* where Humpty-Dumpty claims to be able to give a word any meaning he wishes. The scholars use the example to insist that people cannot simply give whatever meaning they want to words willy-nilly.[8] And of course, if people using those words want to be understood by others, that is true. But it is true not because words magically or metaphysically have their meaning within themselves or because texts can control their interpretation. It is true because language is social. The meanings of words are products of social consensus. We take words to mean certain things because we assume a social consensus or agreement about how we will take the words, which demonstrates not that words or texts contain their own meaning or can control their own interpretation, but that meaning is the result of socially learned assumptions about language. The meaning is here still a social product, a product produced, that is, by human beings.

Finally, this notion that meaning is produced by communal consensus explains why scholars are wrong when they cry that if readers create meaning, we will be plunged into absolute chaos. People, such scholars fear, will interpret texts in whatever way they wish. Texts will come to have literally any meaning, and therefore no meaning in any socially useful way. In the worst-case scenario, people will be able to use texts in unethical ways and even violently. In spite of the fact that this sort of hysterical rhetoric occurs so frequently, it is completely wrong, precisely because of the fact, explained above, that texts as linguistic objects are social, as is language. We human beings are able to read only in ways we have learned, and we have learned those ways in human society. We therefore cannot make texts mean literally anything. We can individually make texts have only those meanings that are imaginable to us, and our imaginations are to some extent constrained by human culture and our socialization into the particular cultures we inhabit. Furthermore, we human beings can affect the ways other human beings read texts. The text cannot constrain readings of itself, but human beings can exercise a lot of influence over how other human beings interpret texts.

This is the constraint on interpretation: not from the inanimate text, but from very animate human society. Chaos of interpretation never actually happens for the same reasons that absolute chaos doesn't occur in our societies: human beings control it. The way people will be constrained from unethical interpretations of texts will never be by the text exercising control over how it is interpreted, but by other human beings exercising such control. The only defense against unethical or violent uses of texts will have to come from human, not textual, agency. That is the way it has always been. This point also suggests that we should be especially diligent about our own and others' interpretations of texts: since the text itself is powerless to preclude unethical interpretations, it is up to us.

None of these (admittedly rather commonsensical) objections has overturned the basic observation that texts do not create meaning; people create meaning. We can, of course, continue using certain ways of speaking about authors, texts, and meanings. We may imagine an author with intentions as one way of guiding our interpretations. We may talk about "what the text says." We may refer to "the world revealed or created by this text." None of these expressions need be avoided. What must be avoided is allowing those metaphors of agency to fool us into forgetting our own agency in the construction of meaning in the reading activity. We must not allow human agency to be masked by the metaphorical or mythical agency of the text itself. Human beings must take responsibility for their interpretations. With this realization, we can enter into discussions of the meaning of Scripture with more sophistication and freed from misleading metaphors of meaning.

INTERPRETING SCRIPTURE

I have been arguing that common experiences we have all had in interpreting texts and other objects we take to be significant should convince us that "texts don't mean; people mean with texts." The same point can be made by observing how Christians have interpreted and do interpret Scripture.

For Christians, one of the most important scriptural texts has been Psalm 22. What, though, is its meaning and how do we find it?

My God, my God, why hast thou forsaken me? . . .
All they that see me laugh me to scorn. . . .
He trusted on the LORD that he would deliver him:
Let him deliver him, seeing he delighted in him. . . .
I am poured out like water, and all my bones are out of joint. . . .
For dogs have compassed me: the assembly of the wicked have inclosed me:
They pierced my hands and my feet. . . .
They part my garments among them, and cast lots [for my clothes].[9]

Few people of our culture, even non-Christians, can read these lines and not think they refer to the crucifixion of Jesus. The Gospels make rich use of Psalm 22 to interpret and portray the crucifixion. But is that a correct interpretation of the psalm?

From the point of view of historical criticism, no. The historical critic, if she or he is behaving like a proper historical critic, will treat the psalm as a product of ancient Israelite or pre-Christian Jewish culture. The historian may note that, in the Psalter, Psalm 22 is attributed to David, but that scholars tend to take such attributions with a grain of salt. The titles and attributions attached to particular psalms seem to have been placed there later by editors of the collection at various stages and were probably not part of the original version of the text. But the historical critic will have no problem admitting that perhaps David, as a leader considered righteous but sometimes persecuted, could be taken as the type of figure speaking the lament. The historical critic may attempt to imagine an author of the psalm, or perhaps simply treat it as an anonymous piece of ancient Israelite poetry. But the primary meaning of the text, its historical-critical meaning, will be one that would make sense in a pre-Christian ancient context. For the historian, the psalm cannot be taken as referring to the American president, but it also cannot be taken as intentionally referring to the crucifixion of Christ.

Does that mean that the Gospel writers were wrong to take the psalm as a reference to Jesus' crucifixion? Have Christians throughout the centuries been wrong to read Psalm 22 as speaking about the crucifixion of Christ? A medieval theologian would say that even if the human author of the psalm did not foresee the fulfillment of his words in the crucifixion, that need not prohibit us from taking the psalm as a prophecy of the crucifixion. The medieval theologian may well point out (as several of them actually did) that, theologically speaking, the author of Scripture is ultimately not that ancient human author, but God. And God surely intended the text to contain more meaning than the limited original author could have imagined. So the theologian may well say that the meaning of the text coheres with the author's intention, as long as that author is understood to be God and not the human author. Or the theologian may not bring authorial intention into the discussion at all, but simply insist that Scripture has many meanings, and one of them, in fact in this case the most important meaning, is the foreshadowing of the crucifixion. Or a Christian could argue that through divine providence—without reference to intention either human or divine—later Christians legitimately derive correct Christian meanings from pre-Christian texts. My goal is in the end not to argue for divine intention as providing the meaning of the scriptural text (though that was a common pre-modern theological claim), but just to point out that there have been and may well be many other ways to think about the Christian meaning of a text of Scripture apart from the intentions of the original human author. For Christians, the meaning of the psalm is not limited to the intentions of the human author, nor is it located merely in the ancient past. Scripture lives in different and constantly new meanings in the readings of Christians led by the Holy Spirit.

Similar examples may be taken also from the New Testament. From the point of view of respectable historical criticism, it is a mistake to read New Testament authors as teaching an explicit and orthodox doctrine of the Trinity. In fact, some of their writings sound so un-Trinitarian that they would have been treated as heretics in later ages. Paul, for example, innocently portrays Christ as "subordinate" to God the Father, a view that would later be declared heretical. In 1 Corinthians 11:3, Paul takes God to be the "head" of Christ in the same way that Christ is the "head" of man and man is the "head" of woman. The hierarchy of God-Christ-man-woman is clear, though such an interpretation would later be considered heretical in its implicit Christology. In 1 Corinthians 15:24, 28, Paul insists that in the time of the resurrection, Christ will subdue "every ruler and every authority and power" under himself, and then the Son will be subjected also to "him," to "God," referring to God the Father. Again, read historically, the text reflects a form of subordination that would make later Trinitarians very uncomfortable. What Paul says about Christ aside, although Paul's own understanding of the "spirit" is rather hard to clarify, Paul never comes close to treating the spirit in the later terms of orthodox Trinitarian doctrine, as the third person of the Trinity.

In my view, however, none of these historical "facts" should dissuade Christians from reading the Bible in Trinitarian terms. Christians have legitimately refused to limit the meaning of Scripture to its supposed original meaning locked in the ancient past, or to the meaning thought to be intended by the original author. The meaning of Scripture cannot be so circumscribed.

MISTAKEN THEOLOGICAL ARGUMENTS
FOR THE NECESSITY OF HISTORICAL CRITICISM

Most of the time, scholars and students give no theological reasons for why they believe historical criticism is necessary for interpretation of the Bible, but

a few have attempted to propose rationales supporting their belief that historical criticism is not only a helpful means of interpreting Scripture, but an
essential one. Careful analysis of these arguments, however, shows that they
don't stand up to critical scrutiny.

The most common reason given for the necessity of historical criticism
insists that Christianity is a historical religion and therefore must be studied
using modern historical methods. It is seldom clear precisely what is meant by
calling Christianity a historical religion. Does this imply that other religions
are not historical? And what could that possibly mean? It would seem that
since all religions have arisen in particular places and times, have spread or
grown in particular historical periods, all religions would be considered historical. And there is no particular reason that a religion, just because it arose
in history, must have its authoritative texts or Scripture submitted to the analysis of modern historical criticism, a method that, after all, itself arose only in
the modern period and long after these religions had been flourishing quite
well for centuries. If historical criticism is necessary for studying historical religions, how does one explain the happy existence of those religions before the
rise of historical criticism?[10]

Usually, calling Christianity a historical religion is meant to point out that
the foundation of Christianity, its originary event, was the life and death and
possibly (according to whether one takes it as a historical event) resurrection
of Jesus. Or scholars may claim that the central focus of faith in Christianity
is the incarnation, which was an event that occurred at a particular time and
place in the past. Therefore, since the foundation of Christianity (in the incarnation or crucifixion or resurrection) was a historical event, the central texts
of Christianity must be studied using modern historiographical methods.

This argument is mistaken for a simple but usually ignored reason: scholars making this kind of argument are confusing two different meanings of the
word "historical" or "history." They are using the term "history" in two different ways. In common English, the word "history" may refer simply to "the
past." We may say that the Civil War was something that happened "in history," by which we mean "in the past." In that sense, of course, the life of Jesus
of Nazareth occurred in the past and therefore may be considered historical.
But when modern historians say that an event is "historical," they are often
using the term in a more limited, technical sense. To call an event "historical"
in this sense means that its occurrence and meaning may be constructed using
the common methods of modern historiography. In fact, philosophers of history (those who study how scholars actually conduct historiographical
research and the writing of histories), when they are being especially careful,
will use the term "history" to refer not to an event that occurred in the past,
but to the constructed account of the past.[11] "History," in this more technical

sense, refers to the accounts produced by modern historians, not to the past in itself. After all, the past no longer exists. We cannot see it at all. We cannot find it in nature, even by means of historiographical research. When a historian, for example, constructs a history of the Civil War, she or he is obviously not re-creating the entire event of the Civil War—that would necessarily require the full number of years of the war to reenact—but only a written account of some of the many different real events that truly made up the Civil War. Here, "history" does not refer to all that happened, only to what the historian writes about whatever happened. The past should not be naively equated with history, which refers to an account of the past, a narrative that purports to depict something about the past, not the past itself.

Notice how this distinction of modern philosophy of history is helpful for cutting through some confusion surrounding claims that Christianity is based on historical events. Christianity is not based merely on the idea that Jesus of Nazareth was a historical person, that is, a person about whom modern historians can study and write. Christianity is rather based on the claim of faith that "in Christ God was reconciling the world to himself" (2 Cor. 5:19), or that Jesus was the incarnate son of God, or that the incarnation occurred two millennia ago in Palestine. The faith that founds Christianity is not based on the mere historical fact of the existence of Jesus of Nazareth or his life and death. It is rather based on the claim that Jesus was divine. These theological claims can be neither confirmed nor denied by modern historiographical methods. Modern historians, when practicing the common procedures affirmed by that modern discipline, can say nothing about whether God was in Jesus or not. The incarnation, therefore, is not a historical fact in the more technical sense of the term "historical"— that is, an event in the past that can be confirmed and studied by normal historiographical methods. When scholars argue that Christianity is based on a historical event because it is based on the incarnation, they are really saying that Christianity is based on an event in the past, but if they mean the incarnation can be confirmed by normal historiographical methods, they are mistaken.

So the incarnation may be historical if by that we mean that it happened in the past. But it is not historical if by that we mean that it can be proven by the typical methods of modern historians. Christians, of course, may well feel that their faith does not need such confirmation from modern historians. Note that there are two separate but related points here: (1) historiography can neither confirm nor deny the reality of the incarnation, nor can it provide its meaning; and (2) Christians do not need the confirmation of modern historiography in order to believe in the incarnation or interpret it meaningfully for their lives. History simply cannot establish the truth or the meaning of the central claims of Christian faith. Historical criticism, therefore, is not necessary for confirming or understanding, Christianly, the foundational events of Christianity.

A second argument attempting to give a theological reason for the necessity of historical criticism for studying the Bible is the claim that the church, throughout the centuries, has always affirmed that a, if not *the*, primary meaning of Scripture is the literal sense of Scripture, the *sensus literalis*, and that the church has always considered the literal sense to be identical to the original intention of the human author.[12] Therefore, because the original human author existed long ago in the past, we need to use the methods of historiography to ascertain what we may say about his original intentions. This argument is correct in its first part but mistaken in its second part.

Christian theologians have often taken the literal sense to be the primary meaning of Scripture.[13] Even when they believed that typological or allegorical readings of Scripture were proper, they usually taught that those readings should not contradict the literal sense. *Sensus literalis* has been a commonly accepted primary meaning of Scripture. But the second claim—that what premodern theologians meant by "literal sense" was the intentions of the original human author—is completely incorrect. As many studies in the past several years have shown, church fathers and theologians such as Augustine, Thomas Aquinas, Nicholas of Lyra, and many others did urge that the literal sense should be primary, and they did acknowledge that there was such a thing as the intention of the human author, but they did not equate the two meanings. They rather taught that the real author of Scripture, as I mentioned above, was God or the Holy Spirit. God or the Spirit may have intentionally put a meaning in Scripture that was not intended by the human author.[14] For premodern Christian theologians, the literal sense of Scripture referred to the divine intention, not merely the human intention. Therefore, to claim that what those theologians meant by the "literal sense" is the same thing we moderns mean by the author's intention is completely wrong. And of course, since historical criticism can say nothing about God's intentions for the meaning of Scripture, historical criticism is not necessary from a theological point of view for the Christian reading of the Bible.

In my view, the most compelling argument against those who claim that historical criticism is necessary for a Christian reading of the Bible is to point out that historical criticism is a relatively recent invention and Christians throughout many centuries have read Scripture in quite Christian ways without historical criticism. Historical criticism, in the sense I defined it in chapter 1 above, was invented and promoted only beginning in the nineteenth century. It became the dominant method for biblical studies taught to students in theological education only in the twentieth century. Therefore, Christians for most of the history of Christianity have not used the historical-critical method in their readings of the Bible. To insist that historical criticism is necessary for the Christian reading of Scripture is to say that no Christian before the modern period read Scripture Christianly.

Such a claim would not only be merely ironic and self-centered, but is also theologically offensive. It offends a central Christian theological belief: the affirmation of the communion of saints. In the Apostles' Creed, Christians confess to believe in "the communion of saints," referring to all Christians living now or who have ever lived. To affirm the doctrine of the communion of saints is to affirm that we accept all Christians as members with us in the body of Christ that has existed throughout all ages and exists now throughout the earth. For modern Christians to say that modern historical criticism is necessary for the Christian interpretation of the Bible is to say that all premodern Christians or those Christians throughout the world today who do not use historical criticism did not and are not reading Scripture Christianly, and that offends the theological notion and the confession of faith in the communion of saints. To insist that historical criticism is indispensable for interpreting the Bible in a Christian manner is modernist imperialism.

Of course, one could argue that even if historical criticism is a practice of reading about which Christians in the past knew nothing—and that most living Christians around the world actually do not practice today—nonetheless there are valid theological reasons for requiring that the historical meaning of the text be the foundational meaning of Scripture. One could claim, for instance, that since times have changed, methods of reading Scripture must also change. But I would counter that if Christians today insist that historical criticism is necessary for interpreting Scripture, they should provide just such a compelling theological rationale for that claim. In my opinion, no such compelling theological argument has yet been forthcoming, and I doubt one is possible. I believe it is much more legitimate to align ourselves with our Christian brothers and sisters of the first eighteen centuries of Christianity, and with the vast majority of those now existing, and realize that though historical criticism may be a useful tool, to teach that it is necessary for the reading of Scripture is unsupportable.

CONCLUSION

The main point of most of this book is to argue that theological schools are generally not doing a very good job of teaching theological interpretation of Scripture and that they can and should do better. I also argue, however, that since students—these future leaders of churches—will spend much of their lives reading and interpreting texts, they should be educated to think in more conscious and sophisticated ways about what sorts of things texts are and how they are read and interpreted. Students need training in literary and textual theory.

Aided by such training in theory of interpretation, students could, for one thing, be better equipped to see through the false claims made by some scholars that historical criticism must be given a central and privileged place in Christian reading of the Bible. They would also be better equipped to imagine more expansive ways of interpreting Scripture Christianly.

I have also hinted in this chapter that we should pay attention to how Christians in premodern times thought about and interpreted Scripture. The following chapter attempts to illustrate, through a few brief examples, how premodern biblical interpretation may be used to nurture and shape new imaginations for ourselves in scriptural interpretation.

3

Premodern Biblical Interpretation

Before the modern period—certainly before the Reformation, and to some extent even before the nineteenth century—Christians read and interpreted Scripture quite differently from the ways most modern Christians do, at least most Christians in North America and Europe. By the term "premodern," I mean those people in the ancient Greco-Roman world, the patristic world of late antiquity, and the world of medieval Europe. To many modern people, premodern interpretations have sounded capricious, arbitrary, and even self-serving. I believe, along with an increasing number of scholars, that premodern scriptural interpretation was anything but arbitrary, that it was the product of the employment of skills learned in important socialization, and that it is something from which we "postmodern" Christians may learn quite a lot.

I do not supply here a general account or survey of premodern scriptural interpretation. Those are available elsewhere.[1] Instead, I have chosen a few examples, in fact some of the most famous examples, to illustrate different ways premodern Christians interpreted Scripture, and I do so hoping to convince other Christian students and educators that more in-depth knowledge of premodern interpretation may expand our own Christian imaginations. As we delve into these interpretations, perhaps we may imagine what it would be like for us to see the text as these earlier readers saw it, what it would be like to interpret the text in the same or similar ways. Perhaps by learning from our Christian forebears, we may escape what has become for many people the prison house of modernism and historical criticism.

The first thing to note about premodern, "Christian" interpretation of Scripture is that it begins with the authors of the New Testament itself, and even with Jesus.[2] The Gospels do not often present Jesus as commenting on Scripture, but as we might expect, when Jesus does interpret Scripture in the

Gospels, he exercises what from a modern point of view is quite a bit of free-dom. When he is questioned about divorce, for example, Jesus breaks one of the cardinal rules of textual interpretation taught in the ancient world as well as the modern: interpret the obscure by reference to the clear.[3] According to Mark's version of the confrontation, when the Pharisees ask Jesus whether it is "lawful for a man to divorce his wife" (Mark 10:2), Jesus first asks them what Moses had commanded. They note that Moses permitted divorce (see Deut. 24:1–4). In an apparent rejection of that clear scriptural permission, Jesus instead quotes Genesis 1:27, "God made them male and female," and Gene-sis 2:24, "For this reason a man shall leave his father and mother and be joined to his wife, and the two shall become one flesh." Note that neither text, taken literally and in its historical context, says anything at all about divorce or remarriage. Yet Jesus is presented as passing over a clear text that allowed divorce and remarriage, and instead interpreting a text that says nothing explicit about divorce at all, and he then reads it as a prohibition of divorce and remarriage. This sort of setting up of one scriptural text to correct or nullify another was not at all uncommon in the ancient world, nor is it uncommon today. But it hardly plays by the rules of modern historical criticism.

Paul was also quite creative in his interpretations of Scripture.[4] In one famous example, Paul reads the account of the wilderness journeys of the peo-ple of Israel as a type for the current experiences of his Gentile converts (1 Cor. 10:1–13). The ancient Israelites, rescued from bondage in Egypt, were "bap-tized" in the "cloud and sea" into Moses. The manna they ate was "spiritual food," and from the rock they drank "spiritual drink." The rock itself, which Paul portrays as following the Israelites in the wilderness (a detail not found in our text of the wilderness wanderings), was Christ himself. Paul thus inter-prets the texts of Exodus to signify Christian experiences such as baptism, the eucharist, and the provisions of Christ to the church.

In an even more famous account, Paul offers an interpretation of the mean-ing of Hagar and Sarah from Genesis that is certainly counterintuitive from a modern point of view, and probably was counterintuitive to many of Paul's ancient readers as well (Gal. 4:21–31). One may have expected Sarah, Abra-ham's "free" wife, to represent the Jews, and Hagar, Abraham's slave, to rep-resent Gentiles. But Paul reverses such expectations, interpreting Hagar to represent Mount Sinai (the site of the giving of the Jewish law) and the "pres-ent Jerusalem." Hagar, therefore, though often traditionally taken as the mother of the Arabs or non-Jews, is interpreted by Paul to represent those Jews who have not accepted Jesus as the Messiah, and Sarah and Isaac, the forebears of the Jews, are taken as the ancestors of Christ-believing Gentiles.

Many more examples of scriptural interpretation in the New Testament are ready at hand. We may think, for instance, of the way the Gospel of Matthew interprets Moses as something of a type of Christ: as Moses was saved from the slaughter of innocent babies by Pharoah, so Jesus is saved, by going to Egypt, from Herod's slaughter of the innocents; as Moses delivered the law from a mountain, so Jesus interprets the law in his Sermon on the Mount. Or we could study the Letter to the Hebrews, which is in fact a sermon consisting almost entirely of typological or allegorical interpretations of psalms and texts describing the tabernacle and its liturgies. But these examples are sufficient to illustrate the point: "Christian" interpretation of Scripture begins in the New Testament itself; New Testament authors provide instructive examples of premodern exegesis, and I urge that we Christians today learn from their examples. But I turn now from those earliest examples of Christian interpretation in order to offer a brief survey of late ancient and medieval readings of Scripture, with the hope that these illustrations may spur our imaginations further for revising our own interpretive assumptions and techniques.

ORIGEN

Generally regarded nowadays as one of the most learned and brilliant of biblical interpreters in the history of Christianity, Origen (ca. 185–ca. 254) has not always been admired. In the ancient world he was much read but little praised, and in the modern world he is much praised but little read. Attention to his works suffered for many years from the taint on his reputation as supposedly unorthodox that accrued to him beginning in the fourth century. Yet until the modern era, he always exerted some influence on later biblical exegesis if only because of the huge impact he had exerted on certain church fathers unanimously accepted as completely orthodox, such as Ambrose and Jerome. In the twentieth century, Origen's reputation experienced a significant rehabilitation, as many scholars, Christian as well as non-Christian, promoted Origen extensively, using him as an excellent example of early Christian exegesis and commentary, and without feeling the need either to defend him indiscriminately or to reject him completely. His interpretations are so learned and creative that they merit, people increasingly acknowledge, much more attention.

Origen is famous for having advocated different meanings or senses of Scripture or levels of interpretation. Perhaps the best known of his comments is from *On First Principles* 4.2.4, where he says that Scripture, like a human person, consists of body, soul, and spirit. The "flesh" or "body" of Scripture is its "obvious interpretation." The soul of Scripture is its meaning as discerned by the Christian who has made some progress in the faith, and the spirit will be discerned by "the man who is perfect."[5] It should be obvious that these are not really definitions of three different meanings found within Scripture, nor of three different methods of reading. The comments refer rather to the level of wisdom and accomplishment of the reader.

Also, it should be constantly kept in mind that Origen was seldom rigorous in using precisely these terms for the three meanings, nor in maintaining three distinct senses, nor even in maintaining three rather than two senses. Origen's practices of interpretation, in fact, are remarkably fluid, creative, and adapted to the particularities of the text in question and the situation of writing—for example, whether in a sermon, commentary, or other usage. Joseph Lienhard explains:

> In practice, Origen prefers other terms for the senses of Scripture, for example: historical, mystical, and allegorical; literal, mystical, and moral; the letter, the spirit, and the moral point. More often, though, Origen writes of only two senses of Scripture, and calls them the letter and the spirit, the literal meaning and the spiritual meaning, the flesh and the spirit, or the carnal meaning and the spiritual meaning.[6]

Origen's programmatic and theoretical statements about the different senses of Scripture in *First Principles* or elsewhere should be tempered by the observation of how Origen actually interprets texts, and the variety of ways he does so.

It has also increasingly been recognized how important the schooling system of ancient rhetoric is for putting Origen's interpretive methods into the context of ancient culture more generally. All ancient readers who were able to read something as complex as the Bible would have had both elementary and secondary education of some sort, and secondary education especially was always education in rhetoric. So sometimes when Origen interprets in certain ways that may seem odd to moderns, it is only because we are not as familiar with the practices of Greek rhetoric, commonplaces that would be familiar to Origen's audiences, especially those among the educated. Knowledge of ancient rhetoric helps make better sense of Origen's interpretive moves.[7]

Moreover, as Lienhard points out, it helps us understand something that is part of the very fabric of Origen's interpretations—his laserlike concentration on individual words:

> The way we read the Bible depends, to a large extent, on the way we learned to read. The student of rhetoric in the ancient world learned by analyzing a text word by word, pondering each word until every possible allusion and every conceivable relationship had been wrung out of it. That sort of education goes far in explaining Origen's approach to the Bible, which differs so markedly from modern exegesis. For modern readers, the unit of understanding is the sentence or the pericope; for Origen, the unit of understanding was the word. Again and again, in his homilies and commentaries, Origen puzzles over the meaning of a single word, a practice he learned as a young boy when he was taught Homer.[8]

A little knowledge of how ancient people were taught to read texts and use them for rhetorical purposes goes a long way toward helping us understand the sensibility of Origen's varied interpretive moves and conclusions.

I illustrate some of Origen's interpretive practices by looking at two rather different examples: his homily on the Good Samaritan story from Luke 10:25–37, and his sermon on the story of "the witch of Endor" and the raising of Samuel from the dead from 1 Samuel 28. In the first instance, we see an example of Origen in his spiritual interpretation mode. In the second, we find an example in which he limits himself almost entirely to what he considered the literal meaning of the text. We will also see that what he meant by the literal sense does not necessarily match our notion of what that is.

In his Homily 34 on Luke, Origen first provides the basic sense of the story, which is the command by Jesus to keep the dual commandment of loving God and neighbor. The literal sense is simply the moral lesson to do good to anyone who needs it. Then, however, Origen provides an interpretation he ascribes to "one of the elders":

> The man who was going down is Adam. Jerusalem is paradise, and Jericho is the world. The robbers are hostile powers. The priest is the Law, the Levite is the prophets, and the Samaritan is Christ. The wounds are disobedience, the beast is the Lord's body, the *pandochium* (that is, the stable), which accepts all who wish to enter, is the Church [the Latin text has a transliteration of the Greek word *pandocheion*, which referred to an inn or stable but could be taken literally from its parts to say "receive all," *pandochos*]. And further, the two *denarii* mean the Father and the Son. The manager of the stable is the head of the Church, to whom its care has been entrusted. And the fact that the Samaritan promises he will return represents the Savior's second coming.[9]

Origen remarks, "All of this has been said reasonably and beautifully," but he proceeds to expand on the basic allegory with his own changes and suggestions.

Origen himself doesn't say that the man journeying from Jerusalem to Jericho is Adam or "every man." He rather interprets it to refer to someone who willfully descends into sin. The "blows" the man receives represent "vices and sins." Origen agrees that the priest represents the law, and the Levite the "prophetic word," neither of which helps the wounded man. That job is for the Samaritan, who is "stronger than the law and the prophets." Origen often enjoys taking names as symbolic, and he takes the word "Samaritan" to mean "guardian." The Samaritan is certainly taken in a way to be Christ, on the basis that Jesus, though denying that he was possessed of a demon, did not deny the label "Samaritan" when "the Jews" said to him, "You are a Samaritan and have a demon" (John 8:48). Origen, though, takes the Samaritan to represent also Christians who follow Christ's example in helping their neighbors.

Origen points out that the Samaritan was carrying with him bandages, oil, and wine, which he wouldn't have had, according to Origen, had he not known he would need them for precisely such purposes. This proves that the Samaritan represents the one who intentionally is out to heal the wounded. The story is about the mission of Christ to heal humanity.

Origen agrees with his cited "elder" that the donkey represents Christ's body, the *pandochium* is the church "which accepts everyone and denies its help to no one," the two *denarii* are the Father and the Son. He takes the innkeeper, though, to be "the angel of the Church." Origen concludes his sermon by returning to what we might accept as a more literal reading of the story, though it nonetheless takes the story as teaching a moral lesson: the story teaches that we Christians are to imitate Christ, pity those who have "fallen among thieves" (that is, into sin), and "go and do likewise" by helping them.

Several observations may be made about Origen's interpretation of the text. First, we should note that Origen explicitly mentions that he will offer only two different readings of the text, one we could think of as the literal sense—the basic reading that would be obvious to just about anyone—and the more elaborate reading that takes the text to refer to Christ's salvation of humankind or the individual Christian. Yet all three senses of Origen's classic formulation are nonetheless present in his reading. The literal sense is simply the story read as a narrative: "a man on a trip from Jerusalem to Jericho was attacked and wounded and helped by a Samaritan." The moral sense could be the message that followers of Jesus should be "good Samaritans" and help anyone in need. The spiritual sense is the reading that takes the story to be about Jesus, the cosmos, the spiritual healing of human beings, and the hospice that is the church.

We should also note that none of these readings, in Origen's view, displaces or negates the others. The spiritual reading does not at all exclude a more literal reading. They are two legitimate meanings of the text that complement one another rather than displace one another. What we would call the allegorical reading about the activity of Christ is also a moral reading taught to his followers by Jesus.

Origen experiences none of the anxiety that we moderns might feel about fixing the meaning of the text with one sense. The truth of the interpretation seems to depend not on making sure we have seen some thing that is really there in the text. Its truth, rather, seems to come from a sense of fit: does the spiritual meaning fit details of the text, other texts in other parts of Scripture, proper Christian doctrine, and ethics? No doctrine or particular ethical proposition is founded simply on this text or one of the interpretations. The allegorical reading is an expansion of meaning into other realms of Christian truth, not the exclusion of a literal meaning or the foundation of new knowledge.

This observation does raise a problem, especially for many of us modern readers. If the meaning derived from the text is not foundationally a source for Christian doctrine or ethics that can be used over against other sources of knowledge, such as doctrine, tradition, or experience, but is rather one expansion of Christian meaning along with all others, how can we avoid simply reading Scripture to reinforce some kind of Christian bubble we already live in? We will see this issue recur as we look at how other premodern Christian interpreters read their Bibles. If Scripture is part of Christian culture, rather than the thing that will challenge or change Christian culture, how can Scripture work to correct or reform the church or ourselves?

The answer to this problem is again in remembering the necessity of human agency for the interpretation of Scripture and the advocacy of reform, correction, or change. We may avoid living in our own Christian bubble and simply reinforcing our already held beliefs and prejudices not by seeking a source for knowledge in the independent meaning of the text, but by listening to one another and even to others outside Christianity. We allow others to challenge our readings. We work ourselves to see Scripture always anew. We profit from our imaginations and the imaginations of other human readers, and we trust in the providence of God and the guidance of the Holy Spirit to shake us out of Christian complacency.

We can find guidance for that kind of activity also by reading the church fathers and their readings of Scripture. For example, in my next example taken from Origen, we see him debating other Christian readers of the Bible. We see Origen advocating what may well have been in his day a minority reading of a text, using his own reading to counter the readings of other Christian scholars. As Origen demonstrates, complacency and simply self-reinforcing readings are not, in the end, countered by the text itself, but by the engaged agency of other readers.

Since Origen is famous as a great allegorist (perhaps to exaggeration), it is interesting to examine one of his interpretations that, though literal by his standards, was nonetheless controversial in the ancient church. As a guest preacher in Jerusalem, Origen delivered a sermon on the story in which Saul asks a "medium" or "necromancer" to raise Samuel from the dead for purposes of advising Saul's conduct of a war. The story is found at 1 Samuel 28 in our Bibles, but in the Greek Bible used by Origen, the same book is labeled "1 Kingdoms," so the sermon is variously titled.[10]

At the beginning, Origen explicitly differentiates two different senses of the text: the narrative sense (*historia*, which shouldn't be taken in our sense of "history," but more like the simple meaning of a narrative, corresponding to the literal sense) and the elevated sense (*anagogē*, the spiritual sense, or higher moral sense). We should note again that Origen does not attempt strict, technical divisions of several different kinds of sense, such as "literal, ethical, anagogical, typological, allegorical." He is content to speak here of two basic levels of meaning, a basic one and a higher one.

Origen first explains that some biblical texts seem to have no value at all for most Christians if read in the simple narrative sense. A straightforward reading of the narrative will edify no one. Origen cites as an example the story of Lot and his daughters. We learn nothing useful, Origen insists, from the simple story of incest between Lot and his daughters. For that story to be useful for Christians, a more figurative reading will be necessary. But the story of the medium and Samuel is beneficial for all Christians, even read on the literal level, because it teaches us something about life after death, which relates to us directly.

The passage was apparently already something of a bone of contention in Origen's day. To many interpreters, the story cannot mean what it seems to say on first blush. For one thing, as Origen notes, someone may object, "Does a petty demon have authority over a prophetic soul?" The assumption in Origen's time was that if necromancy occurs at all, it is caused by demons. Others would say that it didn't really occur at all, but was manufactured as a deception by demons. In either case, the story seems to give power to a demon over either the soul or the image of one of the greatest and holiest prophets, and that is unseemly. Such interpreters, therefore, say that the woman was lying when she said she saw Samuel. "Samuel was not brought up; Samuel does not speak." The whole episode is taken to be demonic deception, not a real event at all.

Another objection raised against the simplest reading of the story concerned the implication that Samuel would have been in hell in the first place. Samuel wouldn't have been in the worst of places, hell. He was too holy for that fate. According to any of these interpretations, therefore, the entire story is based on the fabrications of a demon-controlled, lying woman.

In answer to these objections, Origen appeals to a literal reading of the text. The objector to Origen's interpretation, Origen argues, "says things that directly contradict what is written." To demonstrate this, Origen goes on to insist that the voice of the narrative is not simply that of the woman, but the voice of the narrator. And since Origen takes the author of Scripture throughout to be the Holy Spirit, it is the Holy Spirit's voice, not that of the woman, that says "the woman saw Samuel." It doesn't say, "The woman *thought* she saw Samuel" or "The woman saw a petty demon *which was pretending to be* Samuel" (4.7; emphasis in the translation quoted). And the text says, "Saul knew that it was Samuel," not "Saul was under the impression that it was Samuel" (4.7). Origen insists that we first take the text "literally," which means that the woman and Saul really did see the real Samuel.

Next, Origen argues that the prophecy Samuel gives here did in fact come true. The raised Samuel prophesies the deaths of both Saul and Jonathan and the loss of Saul's kingdom to David. "Does a petty demon prophesy about the Israelite kingdom?" The proof that the appearance was not the product of a demon is the truth of the prophecy. Demons may fake prophecies, but they are powerless to know truly the future or to provide true prophecies.

To the objection that such a holy man as Samuel must not be imagined as residing in hell, Origen argues that even Christ descended into hell, to preach and redeem the righteous in hell (see 1 Pet. 3:19). He further says that the prophets preceded Christ into hell to prophesy redemption. In fact, when the woman says, "I saw gods coming up from the earth" (1 Kgdms. 28:13), that refers to "holy souls of other prophets" and even to angels who accompanied Samuel in his appearance from hell. Both prophets and good angels existed in hell (*Hom.* 34.7.1–3). After all, the good people who were then residing in hell needed the services of angels, as do all people, so it was necessary that good angels also minister to the good people in hell.

According to Origen, before Christ came, all dead souls occupied hell, waiting for future salvation. Origen uses the Christian notion of the "harrowing of hell" by Christ, the doctrine that Christ descended into hell to preach to the souls there, to defend the literal sense of 1 Kingdoms 28: no one should object that Samuel could not have been in hell because even Christ went to hell. Therefore, one of the important truths taught by the story of Samuel, Saul, and the necromancer is "that every place has need of Jesus Christ" (7.4). Origen also explains that before Christ opened the way to paradise, paradise was closed to all human beings. Hell was the waiting place for even good persons who had died before Christ. "Therefore, the patriarchs, the prophets, and everyone used to wait for the coming of my Lord Jesus Christ so that he might open the way."

Origen out-literalizes his opponents in interpretation. He insists that the text must mean exactly what it says and say what it means: Samuel was in hell, and he rose from hell to deliver a real prophecy to Saul (Origen is unclear about the extent to which the woman herself truly raises Samuel or whether he comes of his own accord or due to divine power; Origen seems reluctant to ascribe the feat to the woman). But the story is not important for Origen merely as an account of a past event, nor even to make the more limited moral point that people should obey God and avoid the evil example of the disobedient Saul. The more important meaning of the story is as a demonstration of afterlife existence, also for us Christians. This is central for differentiating Origen's literal sense from modern notions. For Origen, even the literal sense (called here *historia*, which is translated as "narrative") of the story relates to afterlife for Christians, "so that we may discern what our condition will be after we depart from this life." For Origen, this is not the meaning of the text understood anagogically or allegorically or "ethically" beyond the literal sense.

Rather, the literal sense contains in itself a lesson about afterlife for Christians. This is not at all what moderns would call the literal or historical sense of the text, but it is for Origen.

After spending most of his sermon describing what he takes to be the basic, narrative meaning of the text, Origen provides a brief interpretation that he calls the "higher" or more "elevated" sense.[11] As I explained above, Origen teaches that before the coming of Christ all souls, good and bad, had to wait out their time in hell. At the sin of Adam, a "flaming sword" had been placed at the entrance of paradise and all human entrance denied. Christ accomplished both the deliverance from hell of the righteous dead and the reopening of paradise. At the time of their deaths, therefore, Christians will be allowed to enter paradise itself. This is the "something more" the passage teaches—the more elevated meaning. Righteous Christians will be allowed to bypass hell entirely, unlike those righteous who lived before Christ. "If we leave this life having been virtuous and good, not weighed down by the burdens of sin, we ourselves, too, shall pass through the flaming sword and shall not go down to the place where those who died before Christ's appearance used to wait for him. And we shall pass through completely unharmed by the flaming sword."[12] The ultimate meaning of the text, therefore, interpreted in its elevated sense, teaches that Christians have the opportunity to pass to heaven without sojourning in hell, unlike even the greatest prophets who lived before Christ. The last will be first. Those hired only at the end of the day will receive the first coin (see Matt. 20:1–16).

Thus, we have seen Origen interpreting the spiritual sense in one passage and what he took to be the narrative sense in another. Even in the latter case, however, Origen's literal meaning would not match what we moderns would take to be the historical, literal meaning of the narrative of the raising of Samuel. Even interpreted literally, the text has fuller meanings, and those directly relevant for Christians, than would pass muster under the scrutiny of modernist historical criticism.

AUGUSTINE

Though not a commentary or homily, the *Confessions* of Augustine (354–430) provides examples of biblical interpretation from which we modern Christians could learn important lessons about Scripture. I illustrate here only two such lessons. First, the dialogical nature of the *Confessions* helps bring out even more strikingly than usual the premodern practice of using Scripture to supply one's own voice in prayer. Ancient and medieval Christians prayed Scripture. Scripture spoke directly to them, not mediated by self-conscious interpretation.

And Scripture, in other cases, supplied their own voices in speaking to God or Christ. Second, they read Scripture not merely as containing a specific truth, but as generating many truths.[13]

Book 9 provides an excellent example of praying through Scripture. Having quit his post as court rhetorician, Augustine retired for a spiritual retreat to Cassiciacum with his mother and some friends. This is just before his baptism, during a time of intense spiritual exercise as a catachumen. Though he had renounced his career as a rhetorician and had decided on baptism, Augustine seems still struggling to find his future life. He struggles by living within the psalms. "How loudly I cried out to you, my God, as I read the psalms of David, songs full of faith, outbursts of devotion with no room in them for the breath of pride! . . . How loudly I began to cry out to you in those psalms, how I was inflamed by them with love for you and fired to recite them to the whole world, were I able, as a remedy against human pride" (*Conf.* 9.4.8).[14] Augustine says he was angry with the Manichees because, by rejecting the Old Testament and the Jewish God, they deprived themselves of the "remedy," the "antidote" that could have healed them. Augustine believes, of course, that David was the human author of the psalms, but that need not prohibit Augustine from taking their words as referring to himself. So a quotation of Psalm 4 is Augustine's own prayer: "When I called on him he heard me, the God of my vindication; when I was hard beset you led me into spacious freedom. Have mercy on me, Lord, and hearken to my prayer."

But Augustine also takes the psalms to speak with more than one voice. So at times, the words are not Augustine's to God, but God's or the Holy Spirit's to Augustine and his friends, as when the Spirit says to them, referring to God the Father and Christ, "How long will you be heavy-hearted, human creatures? Why love emptiness and chase falsehood? Be sure of this: the Lord has glorified his Holy One" (Ps. 4:2–3). Augustine answers, speaking to God, "It demands 'How long?' It cries, 'Be sure of this'; yet for so long I had been anything but sure, and had loved emptiness and chased falsehood, and so I trembled as I heard these words, for they are addressed to the kind of person I remembered myself to have been" (*Conf.* 9.9). The divine voice speaking through the psalm in Augustine's ongoing dialogue in prayer even urges Augustine to use his anger: "Then I read, 'Let your anger deter you from sin' [Ps. 4:4], and how these words moved me, my God! I had already learned to feel for my past sins an anger with myself that would hold me back from sinning again" (*Conf.* 9.10).[15]

This practice of praying through Scripture has of course never died out in Christian practice, and in fact in recent years has been consciously revived by Christian groups and schools attempting to relearn the practice, known as *lectio divina*, "divine reading." Though *lectio divina*, or "praying through Scripture," has been increasingly introduced in some theological schools, I believe it could fruitfully become even more emphasized as a way of interpreting Scripture, as I advocate further in chapter 5 below.[16] It expands the very concept of Scripture beyond the rather modernist notion that the Bible is basically an answer book or source of information.

Toward the end of the *Confessions* Augustine enters into a sustained interpretation of the six days of creation from Genesis. Before getting into that specific interpretation, though, Augustine addresses the question of the multiple meanings of the text. Augustine notes that other Christians do not agree with his admittedly allegorical interpretations of the text. Augustine also grants that one goal of interpretation should be to ascertain the intended meaning of the human author, in this case for Augustine, Moses. But Augustine insists that we ought to accept that the text will be patient of many different interpretations, even within the notion of authorial intention. Scripture for Augustine is full. "Since, then, so rich a variety of highly plausible interpretations can be culled from those words, consider how foolish it is rashly to assert that Moses intended one particular meaning rather than any of the others. If we engage in hurtful strife as we attempt to expound his words, we offend against the very charity for the sake of which he said all those things" (12.25.35).

Although Augustine has to admit that he cannot be sure what exactly was Moses' intended sense in Genesis 1:1, he prefers to believe that Moses intended all true possible meanings. The Scripture is "full," containing, even in the author's intention, all "true" meanings: "I am convinced that when he wrote those words what he meant and what he thought was all the truth we have been able to discover there, and whatever truth we have not been able to find, or have not found yet, but which is nonetheless there to be found" (12.31.42). Unlike modern tendencies, therefore, the notion of authorial intention for Augustine does not function to limit meaning or to fix it.

This comes out clearly in Augustine's interpretation of Genesis 1. He does not deny that the text refers literally to the creation of the world, but he argues for a much expanded interpretation that relates the six days of creation to the existence of many other spiritual realities. First, he takes the "beginning" of the phrase "in the beginning" to refer to Wisdom and the Son, both of which are references to Christ, reflecting the Christian doctrine taken from John 1:3–10 that God created the world in and through Jesus (11.8.10–9.11; 13.5.6). The "spirit" that hovers over the waters is the Holy Spirit, so the existence of the Trinity is taught by the very first verses of the Bible. The "darkness and chaos" refer to the human state apart from the enlightening presence and inspiration of God, "the dark chaos of our inner being" (13.14.15). The "vault" or "firmament" that God places overhead—what we would call the "sky" (Gen. 1:7), in ancient cosmology taken to be a solid, fixed ceiling separating the air below from the waters above the "sky" or "vault"—refers to Scripture. This is a more natural connection for an ancient reader because the text of Scripture would often have been written on vellum, animal skin, or leather, which could also be imagined as a scroll that would be rolled back at the end of time, as predicted in Revelation 6:14 (13.15.16). The solid firmament above the atmosphere, which will be rolled back at the end of time, represents the leather of the scroll of Scripture, whose writing lies constantly above us.

Augustine then proceeds to interpret according to their spiritual sense the creation of each of the six days. The waters placed above the "vault" on Day 2 represent the "angelic peoples above the heavens," who, unlike human beings, have no need of the material "time-bound syllables" of the text of Scripture to discern the Word, God's will; they therefore can afford to live "behind" the vellum of Scripture, unable to read it from that perspective (13.15.18). The sea that is gathered together on Day 3 represents the "bitter" part of humanity, the "unruly urges of our souls." The dry land represents "souls athirst" for God. Their good works for other human beings are the fruitfulness of the earth (13.17.20–21). The heavenly bodies created on Day 4 represent different gifts and abilities given to human beings. The sun is "wisdom." The moon, as the "lesser light," is the ability to put knowledge into words, and though he doesn't here use the word, Augustine, as a former professional orator, is probably thinking of rhetoric. The stars represent other various gifts, reminding Augustine of 1 Corinthians 12:7–11: healing, miracle working, discernment, prophecy, tongues, and so forth.

On Day 5, God creates sea creatures, which Augustine interprets as signifying "holy signs" and miracles, and the birds are "the voices of your messages," all of which are those things that point human beings to the divine. They also therefore represent the sacraments, such as baptism (13.20.28). The animals created on Day 6 refer to the "living soul." Augustine seems to be playing on different meanings of the Latin words *animus, anima, animal*. And he expands the interpretation so that different kinds of animals represent different "impulses" of the soul: gentle or vicious (13.21.29–31).

In a fascinating conclusion to this interpretation of the six days of creation, Augustine again comments on the multiplicity of textual meanings of Scripture. He takes the command of God to "increase and multiply" (Gen. 1:22, 28) as a command to increase and multiply the various "meanings" one gets from Scripture. "Observe that scripture offers us a single truth, couched in simple words, when it tells us, 'In the beginning God created heaven and earth.' But is it not interpreted in manifold ways? Leaving aside fallacious and mistaken theories, are there not divergent schools of true opinion? This corresponds to the increase and multiplication of human progeny" (13.24.36). Likewise, the "fecundity" of both sea creatures and human beings refers to the fecundity of the human interpretive imagination:

Deep-seated carnality and its needs suggest that we take the offspring of the waters to represent signs displayed materially; but the fecundity of our human reason leads us to interpret the breeding of humans as a symbol of truths processed by the intelligence. . . . For I assume that by this blessing you granted us the faculty and the power both to articulate in various forms something we have grasped in a single way in our minds, and to interpret in many different senses something we have read, which, though obscure, is couched in simple terms. (13.24.37)

Genesis 1, therefore, even teaches that we should multiply interpretations of Scripture, following our divinely endowed tendency to fecundity.

BEDE

Origen and Augustine, like most premodern interpreters, do not go to Scripture just to get information, about either doctrine or ethics. They can do that, of course, but it is not really the dominant use for them of reading Scripture. Rather, they claim Scripture as their own voice. They pray with Scripture, and they use Scripture as an occasion for creative expansion of meaning. Scripture is a machine for generating truths and rehearsing known truths. The reading of Scripture is a means of reinforcing already known truths, of emphasizing already acknowledged morals and ethics. The interpretations of these readers are seldom in themselves objectionable, except if one insists that they do not produce what the text says as interpreted by modern scholars, because the text is expected to uphold already agreed upon, consensus "truths" of Christianity.

Bede (673–735), for example, moves easily between what he calls the *iuxta historiam*—which could be translated as "historical sense" but means more like "narrative sense," since Bede would not mean by "history" what we moderns usually mean—and the *iuxta allegoriam*, the allegorical sense, which he sometimes will call the "spiritual meaning."[17] But in either case, he is usually making a rather uncontroversial point about Christian behavior. He can read even a rather straightforward historical book such as the Acts of the Apostles to make ethical points allegorically.

For example, Bede interprets Acts 9:25b, "They let him [Paul] down over the wall, lowering him in a basket," as follows:

Even today this sort of escape is preserved in the church whenever someone who has been enveloped in the snares of the ancient enemy, or in the traps of this world is saved through the defenses of his hope and faith. For the wall of Damascus (which means *drinking blood*) is the adversity of the world. King Aretas (which means *a descent*) is understood to be the devil. The basket, which is usually constructed of rushes and palm leaves, designates the conjunction of faith and hope, for the rush signifies the freshness of faith, and the palm signifies the hope of eternal life. Therefore, anyone who sees himself encircled by a wall of adversity should be quick to climb into the basket of the virtues, in which he may make his escape.[18]

This is a rather typical example of Bede's allegorical interpretation. He uses what scholarship he has available, in this case Jerome's interpretations of the names in the passage. Bede, like many of his predecessors in Christian interpretation, interprets names symbolically. He interprets the text to make a rather generic moral point about Christian faith or behavior.

Bede also seldom passes up an opportunity to interpret numbers symbolically, as in this example, his explanation of Acts 9:33, "He [Peter] found there [at Lydda] a certain man named Aeneas, who had been confined to bed for eight years":

> This Aeneas signifies the ailing human race, at first weakened by pleasure, but healed by the work and words of the apostles. Since the world itself is raised up in four territories, and in this world the course of the year is divided into four seasons, anyone who embraces the unstable joys of the present is as though flattened upon his bed, devoid of energy for twice times four years. For the bed is that sluggishness in which the sick and weak soul takes its rest in the delights of the body, that is, and in all worldly pleasures.[19]

Bede typically, therefore, first clears up any problems with a literal reading of the text, such as some apparent contradiction with another passage of Scripture or some unclarity in the text read literally.[20] Then he may pass along a spiritual reading of the text he has come across in the monastery's library, or come up with his own. This is perfectly sensible because Scripture is understood to be not simply a source of information, though it is that, but an opportunity for Christian exercise.

Bede is confident, most of the time, that the spiritual meaning he discerns in the text was intended by the human author. As he explains in his comment on Acts 9:36, "Now at Jaffa there was a woman disciple by the name of Tabitha, which means Dorcas": "That is, 'deer,' or 'fallow deer,' signifying souls exalted by the practice of virtues although contemptible in the eyes of men. For the blessed Luke would not have provided the meaning of the name if he had not known that there was strong symbolism [*magnum mysterium*] in it."[21] And why wouldn't Luke have been able to discern the same spiritual meanings in his own text that lesser mortals such as Jerome or Bede can see? From Bede's point of view, the community of spiritual interpreters is expansive and inclusive.

In any case, Bede provides a good example for why allegorical interpretations seem seldom to have been challenged: they usually taught truths that were themselves uncontroversial to the interpreters and their audiences. The texts were taken to reinforce Christian truths already known as true. Scripture was part of the Christian culture these readers occupied, not simplistically its source or foundation.

BERNARD OF CLAIRVAUX

With the High Middle Ages (ca. 1000–1250), we enter a somewhat different interpretive atmosphere. For one thing, commentary on the Bible by this time had a rich and long tradition, and interpreters were not loath to use whatever material from their predecessors they had available. Commentary appears, if possible, even more intertextual in medieval interpretations than in ancient. Second, the atmosphere of medieval commentary was pervaded with the interpretation of the Song of Songs, the book of the Bible that received by far the most attention from commentators and preachers throughout the medieval period. Moreover, the way interpreters treated the eroticism also had changed from the ancient to the medieval period, with the bold eroticism of the Song now emphasized rather than slighted or interpreted away. Ann Astell has well described this distinctly medieval recapture of the erotic of the Song:

> Whereas Origen sought to sublimate eros by suppressing the carnality of the Song, the twelfth-century exegetes, impressed by the unitary nature of love, aimed at an organic transference of the *affectus* by joining the literal image of the Bridegroom to its Christological tenor, thus directing the bridal love of the soul to its divine object. The Bride, according to Bernard, is a soul thirsting for God (*anima sitiens Deum*), and his own rhetoric serves to awaken desire in his auditors.[22]

Bernard (1090–1153), in fact, serves as an excellent example of these medieval interpretive tendencies.

Even by the time he writes Sermon 7 on the Song of Songs, having already worked through six sermons on the book, Bernard has not yet moved beyond the first sentence of the Song, "Let him kiss me with the kiss of his mouth."[23] He hasn't even gotten through the full first verse! In fact, for most of the time, he has concentrated on the single word "kiss." He takes the speaker, of course, to be the "bride," and the "him" to refer to the "Bridegroom," God. He first, in Sermon 7, explains why the figure of the bride is so appropriate as a symbol for the soul in its thirsting for God. But as usual in his sermons, the few words, or even word, quoted seem to function as a door, an entryway, through which we pass to enter the vast space of textual echo chamber, like entering merely the side door of a huge cathedral.

That first sentence leads Bernard to quote Psalm 72:25, understood as the expression of the bride, "Whom have I in heaven but you? And there is nothing upon earth that I desire besides you."[24] That leads to a reference to Psalm 103:32: she is so blinded by love that she does not hesitate to say this to the one "at whose glance the earth trembles." But she is drunk, having just come up from the wine cellar (Song 1:3; 2:4). She is like David, who spoke of the "inebriation" of those in God's house (Ps. 35:9). But of course: the power of love is greater even than that of drink, bringing great confidence and freedom. As we know, "perfect love drives out fear" (1 John 4:18).

This is but one brief example of the way Bernard often preaches on a text of Scripture. The explicit intertextuality partly arises simply out of the fact that medieval monks lived in Scripture, especially the psalms. They chanted them every day, many times a day. They listened to them read aloud sometimes when engaged in other activities. We should also keep in mind that most of the time when a medieval monk "read" Scripture, it was aloud or by hearing it read aloud by another. Unlike modern Christians, who more often may read Scripture silently to themselves, or hear it only once a week or so read aloud in church, medieval monks heard Scripture constantly. It invaded their memories and came to constitute the furniture and texture of their minds. It was natural in that situation for one text to call forth another, which alluded to another, which led to still another.

Another factor at work here, though, is a different conception of "what Scripture is" than that held by most modern persons. As we have seen already with these other premodern readers of the Bible, Bernard and his fellow monks took Scripture to be a vast expanse of space, a labyrinth, a maze one entered and in which one wandered around. So it may surprise us moderns where Bernard ends up going in his interpretation in this sermon of that first "kiss" of Song 1:1, but to him and his audience, he is just following the leading of the text into rooms into which they had not yet entered in the first six sermons— in this case, into a room full of angels.

For next Bernard notes that if the bride wants to kiss the Bridegroom, she will have to gain entry into the interior of his home. And how does one do that? By becoming intimate with the friends or other members of the household. And who would those persons be in this case? Why, the holy angels, of course, who are constantly in attendance on God and in the divine presence. And the angels are the appropriate intercessors for us to God, as we learn from what the angel says to Tobias: "When you prayed with tears and buried the dead, and left your dinner and hid the dead by day in your house, and buried them by night, I offered your prayer to the Lord" (Tobit 12:12). Of course, one reference proving his point should not suffice when Bernard can think of several, so he proceeds also to quote Psalms 67:26 and 137:1.

But why all this sudden attention to the angels, when the sermon began as a commentary on the kiss? Because we now see that the subject of this sermon is really an admonition to the monks not to fall asleep during services, and the way Bernard turns the message in that direction is fascinating. He notes that angels, as he has just demonstrated with a few texts, are with us when we worship, joyful when we are ardent, and sad when we are slothful or inattentive in our prayers. "For this reason it makes me sad to see some of you deep in the throes of sleep during the night office, to see that instead of showing reverence for those princely citizens of heaven you appear like corpses. When you are fervent they respond with eagerness and are filled with delight in participating in your solemn offices. What I fear is that one day, repelled by our sloth, they will angrily depart." Bernard does not let the point lie without backing it up with quotations from Psalms 87:9, 19; 37:12–13; Jeremiah 48:10; Revelation 3:15; Matthew 18:10; Hebrews 1:14; Psalm 8:3; and Psalm 46:7.

But rather than just scolding the monks and admonishing them to do better, Bernard inspires them to do so. He does so by returning again at the end of the sermon to the "kiss," to the erotic with which he began. He urges his fellow monks again, as he has so often, to identify with the bride and to desire the kiss of God with her intense passion. "Her desire is to be kissed, she asks for what she desires" (Sermon 7.6.8). By repeating several times the desire of the bride, and calling on his fellow monks to identify with her, Bernard transforms what they may have experienced as the cold duties of the nightly office into the highly charged erotic of the bridal bedroom. The prayer is the kiss. If we are fervent in seeking it, the angels will help us attain it. We will be kissed by our beloved when he finally comes for us in the night.

This medieval use of the erotic of the Song is designed to inspire devotion to God and to teach love, a practice well illustrated by Sermon 9. Bernard begins with a dialogue of his own invention. He imagines the bride sad and weary. The friends of the groom find her in this state and ask what the matter is. Hasn't she received the "kiss of the hand" and the "kiss of the feet"? Hasn't she been accepted back after falling away in sin? Hasn't she received even a "second grace"? Yes, she replies, but she needs more. A lengthy quotation is here necessary to illustrate the ingenious way Bernard, by shifting the "voice" of the speaker almost imperceptibly at first, turns the bride into the monk.

> I cannot rest unless he kisses me with the kiss of his mouth. I thank him for the kiss of the feet, I thank him too for the kiss of the hand; but if he has genuine regard for me, let him kiss me with the kiss of his mouth. There is no question of ingratitude on my part, it is simply that I am in love. . . . It is desire that drives me on, not reason. Please do not accuse me of presumption if I yield to this impulse of love. My shame indeed rebukes me, but love is stronger than all. . . . I ask, I

crave, I implore; let him kiss me with the kiss of his mouth. Don't you see that by his grace I have been for many years now careful to lead a chaste and sober life, I concentrate on spiritual studies, resist vices, pray often; I am watchful against temptations, I recount all my years in the bitterness of my soul. As far as I can judge I have lived among the brethren without quarrel. I have been submissive to authority, responding to the beck and call of my superior. I do not covet goods not mine; rather do I put both myself and my goods at the service of others. With sweat on my brow I eat my bread. Yet in all these practices there is evidence only of my fidelity, nothing of enjoyment. . . . I obey the commandments, to the best of my ability I hope, but in doing so "my soul thirsts like a parched land" [Psalm 19:4]. If therefore he is to find my holocaust acceptable, let him kiss me, I entreat, with the kiss of his mouth. (Sermon 9.2.2)

About halfway through this remarkable monologue, we realize that we are no longer listening to the bride, but to a monk, complaining that in spite of his best behavior he misses the experience of joy that should accompany the fulfillment of duty. "Living among the brethren without quarrel," submissive to his superiors? These are the words of the monk, not the bride. In the course of the speech, the bride has morphed into the monk, and thus the monk has also morphed into the bride.

Having accomplished this identification of the monk with the bride, Bernard proceeds to manipulate its erotic possibilities. He now quotes from the Song again. "For your breasts are better than wine, smelling sweet of the best ointments" (1:1–2). Noting that we are not told who is here speaking, Bernard first suggests that we take it to be the bride, speaking of the breasts of the Bride*groom*, and he asks his monks to meditate on the beautiful breasts of the Bridegroom: "O my Bridegroom, you are responsible; you have honored me so greatly with the nurturing sweetness of your breasts" (Sermon 9.3.4). One breast refers to God's native kindness (or perhaps the subject here is Christ; the imagery is fluid), the other "breast" to his eagerness to forgive. The Bridegroom's breasts not only smell sweet and look beautiful, but they also dispense "the milk of inward sweetness" and "spray the pleasing perfume of good repute" over those present and absent (9.4.6).

But now Bernard changes the image and asks his monks to imagine that the words are spoken by the Bridegroom about the bride. The Bridegroom has heard her request and arrives. He "yields to her desire by giving her a kiss," the proof of which is the swelling up of her breasts: "she conceives and her breasts grow rounded with the fruitfulness of conception, bearing witness, as it were, with this milky abundance" (9.5.7). But here, just at the height of titillation, Bernard again turns the bride into the monk: "Men with an urge to frequent prayer will have experience of what I say. Often enough when we approach the altar to pray our hearts are dry and lukewarm. But if we persevere, there comes an unexpected infusion of grace, our breast expands as it were, and our interior is filled with an overflowing of love; and if somebody should press upon it then, this milk of sweet fecundity would gush forth in streaming richness" (9.5.7). The monk listening has been drawn to imagine himself as the young, voluptuous girl in a state of sexual arousal and then pregnancy. His are the beautiful and well-scented breasts that perk up at the nocturnal arrival of the Bridegroom. His are the breasts that become fully rounded. His are the breasts that even give forth milk!

I do not wish to insist that Bernard consciously intended to arouse sexual or homosexual impulses in his monks, though I also don't believe such a possibility can be entirely precluded, given the medieval interest in desire and even erotic desire. In any case, Bernard ends his sermon by comparing "worldly or carnal love" unfavorably to spiritual love. But rather than playing down the erotic of the Song, Bernard capitalizes on it. And by writing this for his fellow male monks and having it read in the male community of the medieval monastery, it is difficult—perhaps impossible?—to avoid seeing it as not only erotic, but also homoerotic—and transgendering. The monk is led to imagine himself as kissed and fondled by a male poetic figure. His own "maleness" is challenged by being asked to imagine himself as a young girl with breasts enlarged by desire and impregnated. Though he is also asked to use this erotic imagination to inspire him to high spiritual heights of worship and devotion, the eroticism—indeed, the homoeroticism and transgendering—are still dominantly present.

I believe that asking modern theological students to study these sermons—and other medieval interpretations of the Song of Songs, that most popular biblical text in the Middle Ages—could function well pedagogically in today's world. Christianity has too often been taken as attempting to suppress the erotic. The modern reading of the Song of Songs, which takes it straightforwardly as a love song, is one way of reclaiming the erotic for our faith. But the manner of identifying ourselves with the bride in the Song and reading it allegorically is another way. The reading would work in one way to re-eroticize our faith and lives positively. Second, reading it the way Bernard and his monks do could go some way toward destabilizing the rigid heteronormativity of modern culture, especially much of Christianity. Asking male seminary students, for example, to identify themselves in this way with the bride of the Song might at least make them appropriately uncomfortable, if they are completely heterosexual—and affirmed, if they are not. The medieval interpretation of the Song brings the erotic back into our Christianity and could also simultaneously displace heterosexism. It might even expand our imaginations—about the erotic, our own sexuality, and Scripture. A reclaiming of the medieval readings of the

Song of Songs could help us modern Christians think newly about texts, interpretation, and even sexuality, all in the context of Christian tradition.

THOMAS AQUINAS

The most famous medieval theologian, of course, is Thomas Aquinas
(1225–1274), who also centered much of his theological teaching around interpretation of Scripture. Thomas follows his precedessors in believing that Scripture has different levels of meaning, and he usually begins with the literal sense
of the text and then proceeds to expound, often at much greater length, the spiritual or mystical sense, which to us sometimes looks like out-and-out allegory
and sometimes more like providing simply a moral or ethical lesson from the
text. For Thomas, as for these other premodern interpreters, the text does not
have just one meaning, nor even just two (literal and mystical), but many. One
gets the feeling reading Thomas's comments that he expected the multiplication of meanings to have no certain, discernible limit, and Thomas seems completely comfortable with that situation.

A good example of Thomas's interpretive practices is provided by his comments on John 5:1–9, in which Jesus heals the man at the pool of Bethsaida (or
in some modern editions, Bethzatha) in Jerusalem. Thomas prefaces his interpretation by noting that the miracle story itself is only a "visible sign" of a teaching of Christ. The Gospel of John, Thomas says, regularly combines, as in the
sacraments, a spiritual truth with a visible sign, and in this case the physical miracle is a sign of the power of Christ to heal by means of the power of the Father
(see 5:19). The entire story thus functions on two levels: first to narrate the literal healing miracle, and second to teach the power of God in Christ.[25]

In his particular comments, Thomas often follows this pattern by offering
a two-step interpretation, first of the literal sense of the text, followed by some
kind of mystical sense. He explains, for instance, that the pool was called the
"Sheep Pool," noting that the Greek *probaton* is the term for "sheep." He further explains that it was called this because the priests used to wash the sacri-
ficial animals, of which sheep constituted the most common, in the pool prior
to sacrifice. The Hebrew name of the pool, "Bethsaida," he explains, means
"house of sheep." This sort of information (and a bit more I here pass over)
constitutes the literal interpretation.

Then Thomas offers the mystical sense, first by following John Chrysostom. The pool signifies baptism. As the man will be healed at the pool by Jesus,
so baptism heals us. As water cleanses, so baptism cleanses the soul from sin,
which Thomas demonstrates with a quotation of Revelation 1:5 (as worded in
his text): "He loved us, and washed us from our sins." But the passion of Christ

is also here prefigured since "All of us who have been baptized into Christ Jesus, have been baptized into his death" (Rom. 6:3). Thus, according to this interpretation, the pool leads the reader to baptism, which leads also to healing, and to the passion of Christ, supported by texts from Revelation and Paul: a thick texture of interconnections of meanings.

Without either approving or demurring from Chrysostom's reading, though, Thomas next offers a different reading from Augustine. According to this other mystical sense, the pool of water represents the Jewish people, as Revelation says, "The waters are the peoples" (17:15). The waters of a pool are confined to its banks, so the Jews are "confined" by the law, as Galatians teaches: "We were kept under the law, confined, until the faith was revealed" (Gal. 3:23). Furthermore, this is indicated because it is the "sheep" pool, and the Jews were "the special sheep of God": "We are his people, his sheep" (Ps. 94:7). Again, Thomas passes along Augustine's interpretation without explicit approval or criticism. He is quite comfortable offering both interpretations as true meanings of the text.

Next, Thomas explores the meaning of the text's remark that there were five "porticoes" around the pool. Literally, this just states what was the case, and Thomas explains that there were five different porticoes so that several priests could work at the pool at the same time. He then adds, though, that Chrysostom interpreted the five porticoes mystically as representing the five wounds on the body of Jesus. Augustine interpreted them as representing the five books of Moses. Again, Thomas simply provides the two interpretations without further comment.

Thomas then launches into several paragraphs in which he interprets different terms describing the people surrounding the pool—feeble, blind, lame, withered—to signify different states of spiritual illness: blind in their understandings, withered in their affections, and so on. Returning to the theme of the pool as baptism, Thomas enumerates different ways baptism is like the pool. For example, the power of the pool was not in the pool itself but was provided occasionally by the hand of an angel, just as the water of baptism has no power in itself but heals only because of the unseen power of the Holy Spirit. But baptism is also unlike the pool in other ways. "First, in the source of its power: for the water in the pool produced health because of an angel, but the water of baptism produces its effect by the uncreated power not only of the Holy Spirit, but of the entire Trinity. Thus the entire Trinity was present at the baptism of Christ: the Father in the voice, the Son in person, and the Holy Spirit in the form of a dove. This is why we invoke the Trinity in our baptism."[26] Thomas proceeds to give another couple of ways the pool differs from baptism, and to offer further allegorical interpretations of the passage, but this is enough to illustrate Thomas's interpretive methods.

Thomas pulls on all parts of Scripture to interpret Scripture. A quotation of Revelation or Paul or a psalm supports his interpretation of a passage in the Gospel of John. Thomas also borrows from his Christian predecessors, in this case John Chrysostom and Augustine, and he does so without feeling the need to choose one or the other of their interpretations. Apparently, for Thomas the different mystical interpretations may be simultaneously valid. There are multiple lessons and interpretations to be gleaned from a single text, not only the literal and the mystical, but many spiritual and ethical meanings. And this small selection of Thomas's biblical interpretation also illustrates *what* Thomas gets out of the text. In the first place, it is mostly lessons about basic Christian morality or ethics: the texts remind us through allegorical meanings what we really already know: that we should behave ourselves properly. In the second place, read beyond the literal meaning, the text reminds us of doctrines we already know: in this case that the Trinity as a whole is present and operates through baptism. The allegorical interpretations, as we have seen elsewhere in these premodern interpreters, basically reinforce ethical and doctrinal truths that we already know, though we probably do need the reminders. The interpretation of Scripture builds on and reinforces truths also taught elsewhere in Christian culture and community. The text is not simply, as so many modern Christians seem to assume, a source for specific new information.[27] Rather, it seems for Thomas more like an opportunity to meditate on the truths of Christianity and to encourage the believer to Christian conduct.

CONCLUSION

So what sorts of things can we learn from premodern interpretation of Scripture? Much, I would say. In the first place, reading these interpreters helps us imagine how Christians can read Scripture without suffering from our normal anxiety about finding the right meaning of the text. These interpreters enter the space of Scripture looking for new inspiration, ways to think about God and their lives, yet without seeming to worry much that one reading or another may not represent the meaning of the text. By many modern standards of exegesis, they seem remarkably free. These premodern interpreters also approach the Bible with questions and interests, but they do not seem to approach it as if it were simply an answer book. As we modern Christians have increasingly come to realize, the Bible doesn't work very well as an answer book anyway. These earlier interpreters seem not to have expected it to do so.

But more than these rather negative things we may learn, we may also use premodern interpreters as examples to imitate, both in how they thought about Scripture and its very nature, and how they interpreted it. We may come to think of Scripture as something we can live in, as a space we occupy.[28] We may imagine Scripture as something we can pray with, Scripture providing a script or score for our prayers. We may imagine Scripture as speaking directly to us at times, as Augustine did. Like all these commentators, we could imagine Scripture as patient of many different meanings.

In what would be an important deviation from the usual modernist, and perhaps primarily Protestant, imagination, we might learn to see Scripture as less a simple source for doctrine or ethics and more as an instrument used by the Holy Spirit mainly to reinforce Christian doctrine and ethics we have imbibed from several different sources: preaching, liturgy, music, even our parents and grandparents and our friends. In other words, Scripture is seen less as a simple source for what we know as Christians, and more as a resource used by the Spirit to reinforce the gospel that originally came to us from many different sources. This seems to be much truer to Christian belief and practice through most of its history.

Of course, that need not mean, as I explained briefly in the section on Origen above, that Christian readings of Scripture will never challenge traditional Christian teachings or notions. Precisely because the meanings of Scripture are potentially so variable (remember Augustine's points about the multiplicity of legitimate meanings!), just as Christian history and traditions are much more variable than often acknowledged, we still have rich resources for challenging traditional notions that we come to realize need to be challenged. That will require from us a willingness to think anew, an openness to God's guidance in directions we may not have foreseen, and an attitude of hospitality to the presence and interpretations of others, even those with whom we may disagree. My point, as before, is that complacency and injustice in scriptural interpretations will have to be challenged and changed by actual human agents, not by the myth of the agency of the text itself. That is also part of our Christian heritage.

Finally, I hope that we will use readings of premodern interpretation as an opportunity for exercising and expanding the Christian imagination. These premodern interpretations may seem imaginative to us, perhaps to distraction. But I argue that the rich pasts and traditions of the church are opportunities for our own learning that we ignore at our peril. We should consciously immerse ourselves in the great history of scriptural interpretation in order to enlarge our minds about the nature and meaning of Scripture, in order to spark and form a Christian imagination with which to read Scripture anew. In chapters 4 and 5 to follow, I return to the issue of premodern biblical interpretation, offering along the way more explicit suggestions for how that rich history may be incorporated and integrated into theological education.

4

Theological Interpretation
of Scripture

I was a doctoral student at Yale University in the 1980s, during a time when people spoke about "the Yale Theology," some people claiming that there was such a thing, and others denying it.[1] During that time, I used to indulge in a dull little joke of my own making. I noted that theologians at Yale didn't actually do theology; they sat around talking about what theology would look like if one *were* to do theology. (I didn't claim it was a funny joke.)

The little joke did contain a bit of truth. It said something I think was accurate about the theological climate at Yale at that time. But it also implied something about what theology is, at least according to one point of view. In the first place, the professors at Yale who taught theology then did not publish systematic theologies of their own. They wrote more about what Christian theology should be and do, about what kind of discourse theology constituted, about the ways different theologians used the Bible or Christian tradition or philosophy when they did theology—that is, when those other theologians produced systematic or programmatic theological statements or publications. The Yale theologians did spend more of their time—at least insofar as we students could see—talking and teaching about theology as a discourse and a practice than they did truly producing theological systems of their own.

The little joke was true also in what it says about theology itself. It implies, for instance, that theology, at least in the Christian tradition, is a meta-language that occupies a middle space between, on the one side, actual statements of faith or doctrine, and, on the other side, an even further removed meta-discourse that talks theoretically or philosophically about "what sort of thing theology itself is." A statement of faith is (usually) a proposition believed to represent reality, at least in some way. Such a statement may be from Scripture ("The Word became flesh and lived among us") or from a creed ("We believe in one God, the Father, the Almighty, maker of heaven and earth") or simply from the community or the imagination of the Christian ("A loving God would not do such a thing, and I can believe only in a loving God"). Such statements are not yet themselves theology.

But once one begins reflecting on such a statement, one has moved from the first-order level of a statement of faith to the second-order level (the meta-level or meta-language level) that constitutes theology: critical reflection on statements of faith. This may include trying to decide and explain how the statement of faith might be true or false; defending it or criticizing it by using other statements from the Bible, tradition, creeds, or doctrines; or considering how such a statement could be considered rational. Theology is the practice of thinking how a statement of faith or doctrine can be true, or rational, or consistent with reality or other aspects of Christian life. Then people (usually scholars) may proceed to an even further removed level: that of discussing what sort of thing theological language is, what it does, how different ways of doing theology compare with one another. When I said that the Yale theologians didn't do theology, they rather sat around talking about what theology would look like if one were to do theology, I was saying that these theologians were two steps removed from doctrine or statements of faith. They weren't even at the second-order level of "theology talking about faith." They were at a third-order level of "theoretical discussion about theology."

I should hasten to point out that I believe all these different discussions are perfectly legitimate, indeed good and important. I am also, of course, simplifying. I have spoken about statements of faith as if all Christian faith were a matter of making propositional claims concerning beliefs. Christian faith is much more complex than that. Christian faith and life include many more things than propositions, including assumptions, emotions, practices (such as the acting out of liturgy and compassion), and many other aspects of Christian life besides. Good theology will attempt to deal with the complexities of Christian life, not just explanations of propositional doctrinal statements. But if my simplifying can be tolerated, I believe it may illustrate important things about theology. Theology is not itself faith. Nor is it doctrine. Theology is reflection on elements of faith or doctrine. Theology is thinking about how faith statements are true—or not. Or even more accurate: theology is the explanation of how faith statements may be sensible or rational.[2]

THE NEED FOR "ADULT THEOLOGY"

Most people, whether Christians or not, never seem to grow up when it comes to theological thinking. They assume that Christian faith must be rather straightforward and simplistic. So they may assume, for example, that if they are correctly to believe that God is father, that must mean that God is, in some sense, male. Or that if one is to be faithful and confess a belief in the resurrection of the flesh, one must believe it in a straightforward and literalistic sense, or else one should be more honest and just give up making such a confession. Many Christians look suspiciously on people who offer more sophisticated interpretations of such Christian beliefs, as if they were just explaining away more difficult-sounding doctrines by means of some liberal interpretation. And even non-Christians may think that if one wants to claim to be a Christian, then one should accept all the bizarre and unbelievable things Christians are expected to believe. Otherwise, just be honest and give it up!

Much of this way of thinking exists because most people have never progressed beyond a rather childlike notion of what religious belief is. This state of affairs is as ironic as it is unfortunate. It is ironic because those same adults have become much more sophisticated in most other areas of their lives. They believe or assume the same things that they did when they were ten years old in almost no aspect of their lives except religion. For instance, when we were children, we worked with simplistic beliefs and assumptions about good and evil. We expected the world to be a simple division between good guys and bad guys. We expected our parents to be completely good, unless we horribly came to the conclusion that they were completely evil. We expected simple answers from our parents, and usually our parents obliged.

As we grew more mature, we came to realize that reality is more complex than we assumed as children. To have an adult relationship with our parents, for example, means that we come to realize that our parents aren't perfect, make mistakes, and are people just like most other people. We realize that we may love our parents without despairing when they let us down. Similarly about other aspects of our world: in order to become adults and to mature, we learn how to understand the world as more complicated and complex. Our beliefs about reality become more sophisticated as we mature. Otherwise, we would be stuck with trying to negotiate a very complex world through the eyes of a child's simplicity. What would it be like if forty-year-old adults thought they had to believe the same things about their parents and their world as they believed when they were ten years old?

Ironically, though, this is precisely the way most people think about religious belief. Though they have matured and become more complicated in their thinking about relationships, the world, and all reality, when it comes to what they think about God or religious belief, they assume that if they don't believe in the simple ways one was taught to believe as a child, they are somehow being unfaithful to true religious belief. Though this situation is ironic, it is not surprising. There are few places in our societies where people are taught to think theologically in an adult way. Most churches don't do it. Most schools don't do it. So whereas modern adults mature in their views of psychology, personhood, and nature itself, they continue to act like children in their assumptions about God, faith, and right and wrong when discussed religiously. I contend that churches must self-consciously teach their members how to think theologically like adults. But that means that leaders of churches, whether ministers or others, must be taught not only how to think theologically themselves, but also how to teach others to think theologically as adults.

This approach is no less true for interpreting the Bible. Just as the doing of theology is a skill that must be learned if one is to progress from a childish faith to a mature faith, so people must be taught how to read the Bible with mature theological lenses. Theological hermeneutics refers to the practices involved in reading Scripture as guidance and for resources for Christian thinking and living. But theological interpretation of Scripture, in order for it to progress from childish simplicity to mature complexity, must be taught and learned. It will come naturally for very few people. Seminaries and divinity schools thus have the responsibility to teach their students how to think theologically, how to interpret Scripture theologically, and how to teach others to think and read theologically.

WHAT IS SCRIPTURE?

The first step in learning how to interpret the Bible theologically is to make explicit what one thinks Scripture is. Most people do not realize this, but there are many different conceptions or assumptions about what sort of thing the Bible is. How one interprets Scripture, though, depends a great deal on what one thinks the Bible is. Most people, entirely nonreligious people as well as Christians, are tacitly working with implicit—almost never explicit—models of Scripture.

In the church of my youth—a fundamentalist and even, at that time, sectarian church—we were commonly taught that the Bible, or more particularly the New Testament, was a blueprint for the church. The church's organizational structure (who were its leaders? how was the church supposed to be governed? what should be the relationships among different congregations?) was supposed to be read off the New Testament as a builder would read off the way to construct a house by carefully studying and regularly rechecking the architect's blueprints. Congregations were thus governed by a plurality of elders, all male, who were assisted by a plurality of deacons, also male, all on the basis of 1 and 2 Timothy and Titus.

This practice extended even to forbidding instrumental music in worship because the New Testament contained commandments to "sing" (Eph. 5:19; Col. 3:16) but nowhere contained any commandments to play musical instruments in worship. It was unimportant, in this view, that the New Testament nowhere contained any prohibition against instrumental music. It was enough that singing was commanded and instrumental music was not. God had indicated his desire (and, of course, we all assumed God was male) for a cappella music in church by putting that in the blueprint. He no more needed to forbid instruments explicitly than an architect should need to write in his blueprints something like, "Don't use any of the following materials in constructing the roof." The architect needed only to designate that the roof was supposed to be built from wood shingles, and that should be taken to exclude the use of slate. So, the fact that some author in the New Testament said "sing" and none said "play an organ" was taken to indicate that God wanted singing and not organs.

I remember a preacher insisting that since God had instructed Noah to build the ark out of gopher wood (Gen. 6:14, KJV), God did not need to state explicitly that Noah was not to use pine, or oak, or cedar. Had Noah substituted other wood for gopher wood, or even supplemented the gopher wood with pine or oak, Noah would have been disobeying God, and the ark likely would have sunk. Just as Noah had a blueprint for building the ark, so we Christians had in the New Testament a blueprint for the organization and practices of the church.

Now this is a rational way of thinking about the nature of Scripture, but it led to real problems—problems I remember thinking about even as a young teenager. There is no mention of Sunday schools in the New Testament, so some churches in my denomination split off in order to avoid offending God by the existence in the church of Sunday schools. There is no mention of missionary societies or orphanages or other meta-church organizations in the New Testament, so other churches split off in order to avoid participating with other congregations in supporting such organizations. I know of no churches that split off in order to avoid using microphones, hymnals, or printed educational materials in worship, but people did debate the issues. In any case, it is obvious that the way people were reading the New Testament was heavily influenced by what sort of thing they took Scripture to be.

It is easy to see how the model of Scripture I have just described was produced on the nineteenth- and twentieth-century American frontier.[3] The "American experiment" was an attempt to come up with new ways of being a nation as a constitutional republic. Traditional sources of authority and hierarchical authority figures and institutions were rejected in favor of a textual source available to everyone for interpretation. In the confusion of the growing religious pluralism of nineteenth-century America, with a rising cacophony of different and new ways of being Christian—several established denominations of Protestants, new churches, experimental sects, the rise of the Mormons and other new religious movements, all living cheek to jowl in new communities in what was then the West, and what is now the Midwest and South—a remedy for plurality and confusion was sought in an agreed-upon constitution. Some Christians, therefore, took the Bible, or particularly the New Testament, as just that constitution: the Christian version of the U.S. Constitution that founded and guided the young republic.

It is thus also no surprise that the modern world, mainly in the early twentieth century, produced a quintessentially modernist form of Christianity: fundamentalism, with its view that the Bible is historically and scientifically inerrant or infallible. Just as science had come to see itself as producing knowledge about reality by carefully and objectively observing the facts of nature, so many Christians, using that same model of knowledge, saw themselves as looking to the Bible for certain facts about reality, including of course the nature of God, but also morality, history, and nature itself. The first chapters of Genesis were seen as offering an alternative, even scientific, account of the history of nature and humankind, an alternative that could allow—or demand—the rejection of evolution or "Darwinism." Fundamentalists, though, came to recognize that reading the Bible was a rather complicated activity. They knew that there were many different English translations possible. So they came to believe that the different versions or translations of the Bible were not infallible or inerrant; the texts that truly were the inerrant or infallible word of God were those of the original Hebrew and Greek documents.

Bart Ehrman, a famous New Testament scholar and textual critic, in a bestselling book on, of all things, texual criticism, tells the story of how he, as a teenager, was converted to just such a strict form of textual fundamentalism. He was taught in his youth group and later at Moody Bible Institute that the Bible was verbally inspired and inerrant, not in any particular modern English translation, but in the original "autographs" (the physical documents penned by the historical authors). He decided that if the only completely accurate inspired text was the original text, he wanted to become an expert in the discipline that used the appropriate linguistic and historical tools to discover what that original wording was. So he enrolled in Wheaton College to pursue biblical studies in preparation for seminary, and he then earned a master's degree and a Ph.D. at Princeton Theological Seminary under one of the greatest text critics of the twentieth century, Bruce Metzger.

In the autobiographical first chapter of his bestseller, *Misquoting Jesus*, Ehrman explains how, during graduate study and afterward, he increasingly came to realize just how many thousands upon thousands of textual variants there were in the many extant Greek manuscripts of the documents of the New Testament. Though some scholars had insisted that the variations were minor, and those scholars still held out rather confident hopes that through research we could be relatively sure what the "original text" said, Ehrman came to believe that all our editions of the Greek New Testament were in fact constructions of modern scholarship and that we never could really have any certainty about the original wording of the original texts of the New Testament. This came as a severe blow to his faith, precisely because he had been converted from a rather "social" Episcopalian background to a rigorous form of evangelical Christianity that stressed the absolute verbal inspiration and inerrancy of the original words of the Bible. As Ehrman put it, "What good is it to say that the autographs (i.e., the originals) were inspired? We don't *have* the originals! We have only error-ridden copies, and the vast majority of these are centuries removed from the originals and different from them, evidently, in thousands of ways."[4] Such realizations led Ehrman to abandon his faith in Scripture.

Ehrman is quite right to insist that we do not have and cannot discover the original text of the New Testament (much less the entire Bible). It is also understandable if he assumed, in his fundamentalist period, that the view of Scripture he entertained at that time could hardly stand up to the recognition that we have no access to the "original text" of the Bible. If one takes "Scripture," that is, to be only the original autographs of the manuscripts that came to make up our Bible, then the radical inaccessibility of the wording of those autographs constitutes a strong challenge to faith in Scripture. But this is true only if that is in fact what "Scripture" is.

The view that various manuscript versions of the Greek New Testament, and indeed various translations of the New Testament, pose a challenge to Christian faith has been understandable—even possible—only in the modern world, to be exact since the dominance of the printing press in the production of modern textuality. The church more generally, and educated Christians more especially, have never identified "Scripture" with any particular physical embodiment of the text of the Bible, or with any particular manuscript.[5] Ancient and medieval theologians and scribes knew full well that there were many differences in the wording of the Greek of different manuscripts. Every time they picked up a different copy of "Scripture," they were picking up manuscripts that contained different readings of the text. They knew that sometimes the differences were minor, and sometimes major. They may at times have seen that as a problem that deserved an attempt at a remedy, or an attempt at the best reading or perhaps a unitary recension. But they accepted the variation in the wording of different manuscripts of Scripture as a fact of life, not a difficult challenge to faith.

In the modern world, since the dominance of the printing press, we are used to thinking that there is one right edition of every document, and that in most cases we (or at least the experts) can find it. Realizing that Christian Scripture cannot be so published—that no editor or group of editors can deliver *the* right version, edition, or translation—may surprise modern people, but that is a reflection of the confusion about texts and textuality befogging modern people. It is also a result of the fact that most modern people, including most Christians, are living with what is an immature and untrained theology of Scripture.

For this reason among others, Christian theologians insist that no physical embodiment of Scripture can be identified as Scripture itself, the word of God. The Bible isn't Scripture simply in and of itself. It is Scripture, the word of God, when it is read in faith by the leading of the Holy Spirit. Christians have traditionally believed that Scripture mediates truths that are essential for faith, but this is itself a matter of faith. The Christian view (properly) is that Scripture is sufficient, that Scripture supplies us with what we need for salvation, that Scripture will not in itself mislead us to destruction. But this means that the literal sense of Scripture is necessarily true only to the extent of the essentials of faith. The Christian idea is that we have enough of the real words of Scripture to be faithful people, but that belief cannot be verified in the public square of secular empiricism. It is itself a stance of faith.

The points I am making may be illustrated by comparing the relationship in Christian theology between the church universal (the body of Christ) and particular, social manifestations of church. We all feel we can recognize local, socially delineable congregations, and we with all correctness also call these "churches." It is much harder to point out the boundaries of "the church," meaning the entire Christian community. Many Christians regularly confess, especially when they recite the Apostles' Creed, to believe in "the communion of saints," again referring to all members of the body of Christ no matter where they live in the world, and including all those Christians who have ever lived. But no one can point out the physical boundaries of that body. This brings out the truth of the Christian belief that the "body of Christ," the "church universal," is never identical with any physical social group.[6] It is a mystery of faith that "the church" does exist visibly and in reality, but we cannot delineate it by the normal means of social boundary-making. My main point, though, is that the body of Christ, though visible and real, must not be identified (made commensurate) with any particular human social group or organization. It is "the *mystical* body of Christ."[7]

We may therefore propose an analogy: just as the church is embodied in particular, visible, physical groups of people but must not be identified with any of those groups or even with all those groups gathered together, so Scripture is embodied in particular texts, manuscripts, editions, and translations but cannot be identified with any of them, including the imagined "original autographs."[8] The acceptance of a text as Scripture is no less a matter of faith in God than is the acceptance that a particular congregation is one instance of the body of Christ.

I offer the analogy not to move into a discussion of the church, but to illustrate the theological poverty reflected in the fear that ignorance about the original wording of the text of Scripture may disrupt faith in God or confidence in Scripture. The idea that the instability of the Greek wording of the New Testament throws up an insurmountable obstacle to faith in the sufficiency of Scripture for salvation is the product of a particular modern view of books and textuality. I offer this discussion as part of my larger point that there are many different ideas about what Scripture is. There are many different assumptions, often not self-consciously considered, about what sort of thing Scripture is or is like. People work with different models of Scripture, and how they interpret the Bible depends greatly on what sort of thing they take Scripture to be.

I shall not belabor the point further except to mention that there are many other models for what kind of thing Scripture is or is like. Many people, especially in American Protestantism, think about the Bible as a rule book. We should go to it to see what it says about homosexuality, divorce, family, or abortion. If we read it carefully and correctly, we should discover there rules by which to live our lives. In the past few decades, many Christians can be heard talking about the Bible as an "owner's manual." Just as we should consult the owner's manual for our car in order to know how properly to maintain the vehicle, or for suggestions for what to do in case something goes wrong, so we should read the Bible to see how to run our lives according to the intentions and advice of the maker. Both these metaphors are very popular ways of conceiving what sort of thing Scripture is among, especially, evangelical and conservative Christians.

There are obvious problems. If the Bible is a rule book, it is an awfully confusing and incomplete one. In spite of references to the Bible in the abortion debate, for instance, there is nowhere in the Bible any clear, rulelike instruction about abortion, even though abortion was available in the ancient world also. If the Bible is an owner's manual, it needed a better author and editors. Moreover, unlike really useful owner's manuals, our Bible came to us without illustrations. People in debates about sexuality and Christianity might like to have a few pictures making it clear which "tab A" goes into "slot B," but they will look in vain in our Bible for them.

Another common way Christians speak of Scripture is to call it an "authority." Some Christians regularly challenge other Christians by implying that they are not sufficiently submitting to the authority of Scripture. In my view, though, calling Scripture an authority doesn't give us much because it doesn't tell us, without much more elaboration, what kind of thing is here meant by "authority." Is it like a government agency that sets rules for labor disputes? Is it like a scientific expert who may point out evidence but who has no real power to force us to act according to his advice? Is it like a television chef who can make gentle suggestions about improving a dish? The term "authority," though bandied around much in Christian discussions and debates about Scripture, is too variable, and indeed vacuous, to be of much use here unless it is stipulated what precisely is meant by authority and what sort of authority.

A more promising and fruitful model of Scripture is the proposal of several theologians of the past few decades that we think of Scripture as providing, more than any other one thing, narrative or a story. Though Scripture contains many other literary forms that aren't really narratives—there are laws, poems, songs, gnomic sayings, and many other genres—these theologians of narrative insist that those other narratives have still traditionally been taken by Christians as existing within the grander narrative of what God has done in and for Israel and in Jesus Christ for the entire world.[9] Again, one will interpret Scripture in different ways if one takes it to be more like a story than a list of rules or a blueprint.

I have experimented with thinking of Scripture as a space we enter, rather than a bookish source for knowledge. We should imagine Scripture, in my suggestions, as something like a museum or a sanctuary, perhaps a cathedral. Just as we enter a museum and experience both its building and its art as communicating to us—yet without any explicit rules or propositions being heard in the air—so we should imagine that when we enter the space of Scripture by either reading it alone or hearing it read in church we are entering a space where our Christian imaginations may be informed, reshaped, even surprised by the place Scripture becomes for us. As is already apparent, imagining Scripture as holy space we enter—rather than as a rule book or blueprint—will significantly affect how we interpret it. In fact, it may affect what we will eventually consider a "good" interpretation as opposed to a "bad" interpretation. There is much more that could be said about Scripture as sanctuary space, and I have indeed said more elsewhere, but this is enough to offer it as an example of a different model of what Scripture is.[10] The education of people in the theological interpretation of Scripture should begin, I urge, with teaching them to think critically, self-consciously, and creatively about what sort of thing Scripture is—in their own assumptions and in the history and practices of their communities.

SOME METHODS FOR TEACHING
THEOLOGICAL INTERPRETATION

I have complained that, in my limited experience, most theological students are not taught theological hermeneutics—that is, they are not taught in explicit and self-conscious ways how to interpret Scripture Christianly. Sometimes they do learn it, but more by imitating other interpreters or following implicit rules and

practices of their teachers or others. Scholars have recognized the importance
of teaching not only how to ascertain the historical meaning of the text but also
how Christians should move on to the ethical or theological appropriation or
interpretation of the text. With no claim to be anything approaching thorough
or exhaustive, I offer in this section examples of how a few instructors have
attempted to teach Christian interpretation of Scripture.

Walter Wilson, who teaches New Testament studies at Emory University's
Candler School of Theology, capitalizes on the traditions best known from
Methodism that use the "Wesleyan quadrilateral" to think about the relation
of Scripture to other sources of authority. First, Wilson leads his students
through different ways of thinking about the nature of Scripture, different
notions of what sort of thing Scripture is and therefore how it may function
differently: Scripture as witness, canon, inspired word, and revelation. Wilson
explains that the "mode of discourse" one encounters in Scripture (narrative,
law, prophecy, apocalyptic) or the role of the interpreter (priest, sage, prophet,
visionary) may depend to some extent on which "model" of Scripture is being
assumed. Even different perceptions of God or different functions of authority may be determined somewhat by the different notions of what Scripture is.

After thoroughly introducing students to the historical-critical method, but
also including narrative criticism and sociological criticism, Wilson places those
modern approaches to Scripture within the context of the full Wesleyan quadrilateral, thus problematizing any sole dependence on historical criticism. The
quadrilateral proposes four different sources or aspects of authority: (1) Scripture, (2) tradition, (3) reason, and (4) experience. To illustrate the Scripture
aspect, Wilson uses canonical criticism, that is, interpreting Scripture by appeal
to its canonical shape or structure, seeing it as in some sense self-interpreting
in its role as the church's document. For tradition, Wilson has students immerse
themselves in patristic interpretations of biblical texts. To represent the appeal
to reason, he uses Don Browning's book *Fundamental Practical Theology*.[11] And
to illustrate the role experience may play in interpretation, Wilson introduces
his classes to feminist and womanist strategies for reading Scripture. As Wilson
explains, "This isn't merely a survey. There are different methods we employ to
have a rich, full interpretation of a text. The quadrilateral provides a way of
doing this from the tradition of the students."[12]

My next example comes from Charles Cosgrove's book *Appealing to Scripture in Moral Debate: Five Hermeneutical Rules*. As the title indicates, this is not
a book on theological interpretation related to doctrine or faith, but rather a
study of how Christians appeal to Scripture in debates about ethics in particular. The book is useful for my purposes for several reasons. First, Cosgrove
rightly rejects the idea that we can come up with some kind of prescriptive
method of interpretation that would produce reliably Christian readings of the

Bible if applied rather mechanically. As he puts it, "Hermeneutical rules are not formulas; they require judgment, even creativity."[13] Second, Cosgrove's book does not pretend to offer rules for interpretation derived abstractly or somehow from the text itself, from simply tradition, or from some formal ecclesiastical authority, all misleading attempts to ground one's own rather creative practices in some kind of authority outside the messy process of interpretation itself. Rather, Cosgrove's suggestion is that we may learn how to interpret Scripture more critically, and self-critically, if we begin by examining how Christians do read Scripture when engaged in discussion and debate. This is a commendable way to proceed. I use Cosgrove's book to provide an example for how one could teach Christians to interpret Scripture by showing them how Christians actually have interpreted and do interpret Scripture. This is teaching by modeling, and then critically evaluating the modeled practices for the purposes of training our Christian imaginations to interpret Scripture Christianly.

Cosgrove has read through much Christian literature in recent years that uses Scripture in debates about morality. He summarizes the many different kinds of arguments into five different hermeneutical rules. These rules are seldom invoked explicitly. Rather, Cosgrove himself notices similarities in how people read Scripture and how they either appeal to it to support their positions or use other interpretive strategies when Scripture does not seem to support their position. This is not to say that these readers are simply manipulating the text for their own ends. We may readily acknowledge that people sincerely believe the text should be taken to mean what they claim it means. Part of the point of the exercise is to demonstrate that different Christians sincerely read the text differently for different purposes.

Cosgrove's book is not brief, nor is it simple. He spends a full chapter explaining and critically evaluating each of the five hermeneutical rules he identifies. I, on the other hand, must here be brief, so I list the different rules and quite summarily attempt to illustrate each. I urge the reader to examine Cosgrove's study more deeply.

1. *The Rule of Purpose.* "The purpose (or justification) behind a biblical moral rule carries greater weight than the rule itself."[14] Take, for example, the Old Testament law against lending at interest (Exod. 22:25; Deut. 23:19–20; see Ezek. 18:8; 22:12). The reason for the law was to protect the poor from financial oppression, and perhaps in a very simple economic system, the law could have that effect. But in many other contexts, from the economy of poverty in the contemporary United States to India, forbidding any lending at interest would mean the prohibition of proven effective programs that have helped change the dire situations of poor people, by lending small amounts at very reasonable rates of interest. Since enforcing the letter of the law would in the

end work against the spirit or purpose of the law, it is more ethical to interpret the law so as to allow modern lending at interest. In Cosgrove's words, "We reject the rule against lending at interest, but treat its purpose or justification as carrying abiding moral force."[15]

2. *The Rule of Analogy.* "Analogical reasoning is an appropriate and necessary method for applying scripture to contemporary moral issues" (51). Cosgrove argues that the use of analogical reasoning is always necessary in the use of Scripture whenever there is any kind of "gap" between ancient culture and ours (53). But he points out that sometimes the use of analogy in biblical interpretation becomes more explicit. One example he gives is when Christians interpret the narrative of the exodus as teaching an ethic of liberation or the evils of slavery or other forms of oppression (72–81).

3. *The Rule of Countercultural Witness.* "There is a presumption in favor of according greater weight to countercultural tendencies in scripture that express the voice of the powerless and the marginalized than to those tendencies that echo the dominant voices of the culture" (90). Many contemporary Christians are much more likely to appropriate scriptural texts that may be seen as supporting the interests of the poor and weak against those of the rich and powerful. The assumption, whether explicitly stated or not, is that Scripture must teach a countercultural gospel—or at least as countering a culture that maintains the ideological interests of a ruling class perceived as self-interested and oppressive.

4. *The Rule of Nonscientific Scope.* "Scientific (or 'empirical') knowledge stands outside the scope of scripture" (116). Christians will frequently argue that Scripture should not be expected to furnish truths about nature that more correctly fall under the purview of science. Even quite conservative Christians, for example, do not really accept the cosmological geography found in the Bible. If they believe in the existence of hell or heaven, for example, they usually do not believe that hell exists below the dirt under our feet or that heaven is simply "up there," though those were precisely the cosmological locations of those places we find in the Bible read literally and historically. Likewise when it comes to ethics: many Christians argue that the subordination of women to men, or the naturalness of hierarchy and patriarchy—taught by biblical writers as physically inscribed in the cosmos—were products of ancient notions of the cosmos and gender which we need not accept, especially in light of modern science (143–48).

5. *The Rule of Moral-Theological Adjudication.* "Moral-theological considerations should guide hermeneutical choices between conflicting plausible interpretations" (154). Cosgrove shows that this rule was more explicitly used in premodern interpretation. For example, Augustine's rule of love taught that no interpretation of Scripture could be ethically Christian if it violated the

commandment to love God and one's neighbor. Similarly, Bernard of Clair-vaux taught that any interpretation should match acknowledged orthodoxy in doctrine and Christian morality.[16] Cosgrove provides several examples also from modern interpretation, such as liberation theology's privileging of the hermeneutic of the oppressed. In any case, the interpretations that fall under this rule are those that bring to a reading of Scripture other sources of moral or theological wisdom.

Of course, the vast array of diverse strategies by which Christians interpret Scripture for ethical ends is not encompassed by Cosgrove's five hermeneuti-cal rules, as he would gladly admit. And we must keep in mind that Cosgrove himself has not invented these reading strategies, nor does he simply promote them as prescriptions for good interpretations of Scripture. In fact, he consis-tently points out possible weaknesses or potential problems with the use of each rule. The value of his study is that it could make Christians more con-scious of how they themselves and others appeal to Scripture in moral debate. Such knowledge could make our debates more fruitful. As Cosgrove says, "The identification and explication of these rules should, at the very least, reveal why arguments sometimes work and sometimes don't, showing those gaps in assumptions that make us sometimes talk past each other" (11). I offer a summary of the study as one example for how we might think about teach-ing theological interpretation of Scripture: by starting off analyzing how Christians, now and over the centuries, actually have interpreted and do inter-pret Scripture theologically.

Jack Rogers has done a similar study, though in his case he illustrates the use of seven guidelines for biblical interpretation explicitly published by the Presbyterian Church (U.S.A.). The guidelines derive from generally orthodox Christian notions of the authority and interpretation of Scripture, and, as Rogers points out, they basically express principles used throughout many Christian denominations. I would emphasize, though, that the particular com-bination of this set of guidelines owes a great deal to a heritage of Reformed theology and history. In his book *Jesus, the Bible, and Homosexuality: Explode the Myths, Heal the Church*, Rogers appropriates the guidelines to address the con-troversial issues surrounding homosexuality in contemporary Protestant denominations, the Presbyterian Church especially.[17]

After explaining how the seven guidelines were developed and published, Rogers lists them, providing in each case quotations from Reformed sources (such as John Calvin) and confessions that express the principle, and then applying the guideline to the issue of how Scripture should be interpreted con-cerning homosexuality. The guidelines are fairly straightforward, and I quote them as they are given by Rogers:

1. Recognize that Jesus Christ, the Redeemer, is the center of scripture. . . . When interpreting scripture, keeping Christ in the center aids in evaluating the significance of the problems and controversies that always persist in the vigorous, historical life of the church. [I have abbreviated the statement of this guideline.]
2. Let the focus be on the plain text of scripture, to the grammatical and historical context, rather than to allegory or subjective fantasy.
3. Depend on the guidance of the Holy Spirit in interpreting and applying God's message.
4. Be guided by the doctrinal consensus of the church, which is the rule of faith.
5. Let all interpretations be in accord with the rule of love, the two-fold commandment to love God and to love our neighbor.
6. Remember that interpretation of the Bible requires earnest study in order to establish the best text and to interpret the influence of the historical and cultural context in which the divine message has come.
7. Seek to interpret a particular passage of the Bible in light of all the Bible.

Though these guidelines are not especially complicated, much of the value of Rogers's presentation comes not just from the statement of the guidelines, but from his illustrations of how each may be used to address the issue of homosexuality and Scripture.

Rogers is quite clear that the use of these guidelines will not guarantee any particular outcome of interpretation. The guidelines cannot be depended on to deliver even good or ethical interpretations. But he urges that Christians at least may more easily come together in productive dialogue in the face of controversial issues if they can agree on some basic principles of interpretation.

My own interest in Rogers's work here is its function as one example among others for how students could be introduced to the theological and ethical interpretation of Scripture. I do not necessarily wish to recommend it as the way to teach interpretation. In fact, I have fairly firm disagreements with some of the expressions within the guidelines. For example, as should already be apparent to anyone who has read my previous chapters, the rejection of the use of allegory in guideline 2 is, in my view, overly modernist and Protestant. Further, its practical equation of allegory with "subjective fantasy" should be seen as theologically offensive from the perspective of the longer history of Christian orthodoxy and practice. My point in citing these guidelines is to suggest that many different methods could be developed for teaching Christians better how to interpret Scripture. The particular way of teaching theological interpretation is at this time less important for me than the fact that schools and churches need to come to grips with the necessity of teaching it. In the next two sections of this chapter, I offer my own reflections on how we might do so.

INTERPRETATION AS IMPROVISATION

From a young age, I was a musician. From before I can remember, my entire family sang together, even improvising harmonies by ear. I learned how to harmonize in singing simply by listening to my parents. Later, I learned to read music, first on piano, and then, during my teenage years, on trumpet. My goal for years was to become a professional trumpeter, playing in orchestras and jazz bands. Although I had been taught by my family to improvise in singing, and I had taught myself to improvise on piano and guitar, I remember that my trumpet teacher had to teach me to improvise on trumpet. I had learned to play the trumpet first by reading music, and I didn't feel able to improvise freely on trumpet. So when I was about sixteen years old, my trumpet teacher began teaching me to improvise.

I don't know how it is done today, but at that time, improvisation was usually taught by teaching a student certain skills first, different mechanics or tools that could later be used to improvise more freely. We learned all the major scales, then minor scales, then different kinds of minor scales, such as harmonic and melodic minors. For jazz, it was important to learn to play five-tone scales in all keys. We learned to play arpeggios (a string of notes that together would make up a chord) in all keys. We learned from our teachers, or often simply from picking up such things from other musicians, different riffs or patterns of notes. Various small structures of music were learned and practiced until the fingers automatically played them. For the seasoned musician, many different patterns of notes and rhythms become so automatic that one can paralyze oneself by thinking about them too much while playing. The practice of scales, chords, arpeggios, and riffs render them second nature to the musician. But that doesn't mean that the musician has not had to learn them and practice them repeatedly until they become second nature.

Musical improvisation, like improvisation in theater, sets up boundaries within which freedom is allowed—or expected. A musician can't play just anything at all in an improvisation. The improvisation is expected to be in the same key in which the other musicians are playing. If it is a jazz improvisation, it is expected to follow certain conventions. An improvisation by a church organist will have to work within the boundaries of different expectations. The cadenza made up by a classical music soloist in a concerto will work with different forms and boundaries from those expected in jazz or rock music. Improvisation is freedom and creativity within certain socially constructed expectations. The difference between a bad improvisation and a good one depends on a balance of freedom and creativity within the boundaries of acceptable musical forms.

Several scholars have recently argued that theological reasoning, including theological interpretation of Scripture, is like improvisation in music or acting.[18] I suggest we consider explicitly teaching interpretation like teaching improvisation. Students are taught mainly by imitation, just as musicians regularly imitate more experienced musicians. Students learn to do word studies of the Greek and Hebrew texts, compare texts with others, study the sources of quotation and allusion, outline passages and books. But beyond these regular skills and practices of grammatical and historical-critical exegesis, students should also, in my view, be taught interpretations of Scripture from premodern interpreters and nonacademic interpretations of our own time. In my proposal, students would learn just as much from theological and literary interpreters as from historical critics.

In a way, the studies of Cosgrove and Rogers in the previous section of this chapter offer descriptions of the riffs and improvisations of other interpreters. By being shown, in an explicit manner, typical ways that Christians have interpreted Scripture, students learn certain moves they themselves may make in interpretation. So the rhetorical analysis of existing interpretations is like the formalizing of structures of music, such as scales or arpeggios. And by studying such structures, students learn the basic building blocks from which they will then more consciously construct their own interpretations. Too many students have been led to believe that they will arrive at the right or true meaning of the text if they follow certain steps or a particular method. The notion of improvisation better teaches that there is no one right interpretation of a text of Scripture, but that does not mean that all interpretations are just as good as all others. One cannot predict what meaning one will find in Scripture by following a prescriptive method. One must practice creativity and exercise the imagination.[19] But results that are genuinely true and Christian will be those that creatively interpret Scripture within the boundaries and expectations of Christianity. Teaching biblical interpretation as improvisation highlights important aspects of interpretation: that it requires and nurtures creativity, that the "end result" will not be predictable ahead of time, and that interpretation nonetheless takes place within socially constructed boundaries and expectations.

THEOLOGY "IN A SENSE"

As I have already admitted, I have no suggestions for the one good way to teach theological reasoning or interpretation. I have already provided some examples of how others do and could teach theological hermeneutics. I do think we could imagine many different ways to teach students not only historical criticism but also theological interpretation of Scripture. In fact, in this last section of this chapter I introduce a way of doing so that I myself have used.

One could well teach the doing of theology, I believe, by means of a rather simple method. Or, I should say, the method is simple to describe but complicated to practice. One could teach students how to do theology simply by beginning with any statement of faith—say, a statement from a creed, such as "Christ descended into hell"—and ask students to demonstrate, using the different resources from Christian Scripture, tradition, their own experiences, commonsense notions shared with others, or whatever, how the statement could be considered Christianly true. But then, in my view, it is just as important to ask them to construct an account explaining how the statement is or could be false, using the same resources.

From a traditional Christian point of view, one I share, every statement a human being can make, especially about God or theology, is true only "in a sense." And every statement is or can be false "in a sense." A statement is true or false depending on how it is taken, how it is interpreted. Since no statement simply is true or false in itself—precisely because, as I demonstrated in chapter 2 above, it contains no meaning simply in itself—the statement is true only if it is interpreted "truly."[20] And any statement may be interpreted in a way to render a meaning that would be false by Christian criteria. It is important for students to learn that, Christianly speaking, any human statement about God may be both true and false, according to how it is understood and used. I argue that making this fact explicit may lead to an effective way of teaching theological reasoning itself.

Let us take, as an example, the statement mentioned above from the Apostles' Creed: "He [Christ] descended into hell." In order to defend the truth of the confession, students may refer to biblical texts that could be read as referring to such a descent, such as 1 Peter 3:19, or even Acts 2:27 or Ephesians 4:9. Students may invoke and then critically analyze ancient and medieval teachings about the descent, such as Origen's reference to it when he is discussing the story of the "witch of Endor" mentioned above in chapter 3. Students may admit even that they certainly do not believe in a literal, physical space of hell under the ground, or that they do not believe in hell literally at all, but that the confession rather expresses our faith that there is no place where the redemption of Christ is impossible. The statement is true because it says something true about our relationship to God: God's love can reach us and save us no matter where we find ourselves, no matter how dreadful our situation. In these and countless other ways, students learn that theology is the "making sense" of a statement of faith, using all our resources for demonstrating that a faith statement may be seen as rational and true.

But, as I said, students should not be allowed to stop there. They should also be taught to demonstrate how the statement should not be uncritically accepted as true. Almost none of us, for example, believes that hell is a physical space literally existing below our feet, though that is exactly what Christians have believed in centuries past, and quite likely what the authors of our biblical texts intended. We may believe that one need not buy into ancient cosmology, with a three-tiered universe, for instance, in order nonetheless to believe in the existence of hell. In fact, a modern Christian may argue that it is a false interpretation of the confession to insist that it must be taken in that ancient, physicalist sense—to insist that Christ literally and physically "went down."

Other Christians may argue that they do not, and cannot, believe in the literal existence of any kind of hell understood in the traditional, premodern way—that is, as even a spiritual place where the conscious souls of human beings and angels are left to suffer for eternity. Students may make arguments—again using Scripture, tradition, appeals to notions of Christian love or the perfection of God, all kinds of resources—to argue that the confession may be accepted as true when taken as saying something about God's love, but not when taken as insisting on eternal suffering created or allowed by a loving God. In any of these ways, and many more we could imagine, students should be able to demonstrate how the confession "Christ descended into hell" may be quite dangerous and false when interpreted in certain ways.

The exercise described here could be practiced on any statement of faith or proposition. The belief in "God the father" is true if taken to refer to God as the progenitor of all being, but it is false if taken to mean that God must be male (rather than and to the exclusion of being female). The confession that Jesus Christ is the "son of God" is true if taken to mean that Jesus is the second person of the Trinity, but it is false (by orthodox standards) if it is taken to mean that Jesus is subordinate and inferior to God the father. Even statements that seem obviously and always true, such as the confession that "God is love," may still be dangerous or false if interpreted wrongly. The long tradition of negative theology has taught us that any statement about God must be seen as potentially false, since to say anything at all about God may be taken to define God, limiting God's being. Any such limit is false. To put it another way, identifying God with anything we human beings can imagine would be idolatrous, because the identification of God with anything at all except God is idolatrous. Therefore, even statements of faith that seem on first blush to be eternally true should be subjected to critical theological analysis to demonstrate how they could be false or dangerous.

What I have been describing here is, on the one hand, a simply stated method for teaching people how to do theology, how to make Christian, rational sense out of Christian beliefs. I admit, on the other hand, that actually practicing the method is complex indeed, requiring knowledge of Scripture, tradition, history, and culture. Moreover, the practice of this sort of theological method will require skills learned for theological improvisation. Yet the description of the method is not particularly complicated, and the same method can be easily extended to teaching theological interpretation of Scripture. Students could be given the task of reading a passage of Scripture and arguing, first, that when interpreted in a certain way the passage can be seen as "Christianly true"—but then, when interpreted in a different way, it should be seen as "Christianly false," that is, as teaching something Christians should not believe about God or reality.

Take, for example, Genesis 32:22–30, the story of Jacob wrestling all night with a man by the river Jabbok. The story itself has a rich history of interpretation. Christians over centuries have tried to understand even what is supposed to be happening in the story, much less its deeper meaning. Is the "man" Jacob wrestles an angel? or God? What would it mean for Jacob to have a wrestling match with God? And for God to lose the match? Students could be introduced to how modern historical criticism might approach the story, learning that it fits with other ancient folk stories of great men or even tricksters fighting with gods or other superhuman beings, tricking them into a blessing. The students could be led through attempts by the early church fathers to make sense of the story. Students could be encouraged to read the story as a story, as a piece of entertaining literature.

Then students would be challenged: What might be a bad interpretation (from a "Christian" perspective, that is) of this text? They might answer that we as Christians, because of the later development of Christian doctrines of God, should not take the story to teach that God is just a physical, visible man in a literal sense. If the text is taken as disconfirming the Christian doctrine of the transcendence of God, that would be a false interpretation. Other students might argue that taking the story to teach that God really does oppose us and fight against us could be a false interpretation. They might explain that Christians shouldn't interpret the story to mean that we should be on the watch to see how we can manipulate God to give us what we want, as if by our actions we can force God to bless us. These and many other false interpretations (again from a Christian point of view) could be imagined and put into words.

But then students could also be challenged to provide what may be truly Christian interpretations of the text. The story may be interpreted to mean that God is indeed willing to struggle with us, that sometimes our own dark nights may feel like a wrestling match with God, but that God will see us through the night after all. We might even say that, in a sense, God is willing to allow us to win a round now and then. We might take the story to teach that we have a God who allows us to talk back, to resist, to doubt. What makes one of these interpretations right and another wrong is not just some correspondence with an ancient author's intention or that it is the proper historical-critical meaning of the text. What makes an interpretation right or wrong has to do with complex expectations deriving from Christian values, beliefs, doctrines, and ethics.

This is only one example taken at random from the vast resources provided by the entire Bible. Any part of the Old or New Testaments could provide other examples, precisely because the true or false meaning of a text is dependent on how it is interpreted. Examples could be multiplied without end. But as I have pointed out before, so let me stress again: this is not teaching a reliable method by which Christians may be assured that they will end up with *the* meaning of the text. But it is a method by which people may be taught to become practiced in the faithful improvisation that is Christian interpretation of Scripture.

CONCLUSION

Thinking theologically and in an adult manner is important, especially in the pluralistic world we inhabit. I say this not because I believe we should be worried about defending Christian faith from its detractors. I think that most apologies for the faith fall flat and do little to convince nonbelievers about the truth of Christianity. In fact, in my opinion, today the best defense of Christian faith, if any is needed, is simply the living out of a rational faith. Christians need to learn to think theologically and interpret Scripture theologically not for purposes of apology, but rather because doing so will better enable them to find more joy in their faith.

But in order for Christians to learn this, they must be taught it. Thinking theologically, like sex, does not come naturally. We have to learn how to do it, and in order to do it better we have to practice it. Likewise, theological interpretation of Scripture must be taught, and taught better than we are currently doing it. I urge that churches and theological schools must come up with creative ways to teach Christians, and especially those who will be leading churches, to interpret Scripture with theological sophistication.

5

Curricular Dreams

The last question I regularly asked professors in my survey of faculty teaching in theological schools was, "Without paying attention to known constraints or contingencies, could you offer a fantasy curriculum of your own imagination for teaching biblical studies? Would you organize the curriculum of the seminary [or divinity school] differently if you could?" The answers were interesting, not always the same, and in many cases telling.

The biggest surprise for me, I must admit, was how many professors offered no suggestions for significant changes, or they suggested minor changes that would have allowed the basic structure and requirements of their institutions to remain in place. Some confessed to liking their current curriculum fine. Others suggested minor changes. Some would require more of the subjects they themselves teach. Several faculty who teach Bible bemoaned the fact that few of their present students learn Hebrew or Greek, and they wished for a return to requiring some knowledge of either those two or at least one biblical language. Some argued that students needed longer and deeper introductory courses to the two Testaments. Professors recognized, of course, that a theological education already requires three years in most cases and that getting more requirements into that limited amount of time posed problems. They wished, therefore, that perhaps another entire year of coursework could be added to the curriculum. In a rather more creative vein, Ted Jennings, at Chicago Theological Seminary, felt that many students currently entering seminary, often years after finishing college and now beginning what will be a second career, need better general education in the humanities as preparation for the study of religion. He suggested that adding a year of general humanities education—for example, in literature, history, and philosophy—would better prepare contemporary students for the critical and engaged study of their own religions than would simply more requirements in currently taught seminary subjects.

Other scholars mentioned particular subjects they felt should be better emphasized in their institutions. David Scholer, at Fuller Theological Seminary, wished that students—considering our shrinking globe and pluralistic society—had more exposure to other religions, especially though not exclusively Judaism, Islam, and perhaps Hinduism. He also felt that most students would benefit from more education in patristics and U.S. history, with special emphasis on the interpretation of the Bible in history. Deborah Appler, at Moravian Theological Seminary, noted that students these days would benefit from more emphasis on global perspectives, including study abroad. Such suggestions demonstrate that many scholars recognize that the traditional disciplines in theological education may not succeed in placing the understanding and practices of faith sufficiently in the global, pluralistic world in which their students will be ministering.

Not surprisingly, since most of those professors I interviewed taught in biblical studies or theology (two of the core fields of traditional theological education), some faculty called for a de-emphasis on courses in the practical fields, such as preaching, pastoral counseling, church organization, or conflict management. Some faculty shared their belief that many of those more practical skills of the ministry could be better learned on the job by means of working in congregations or other institutions (in field placements or the like). They argued that valuable course time should be reserved for those more academic subjects that require courses (biblical studies, theology, church history, for instance), and that other means of training future church workers should be found for the less academic subjects. Very few, though there were a few, countered that they felt perhaps even more emphasis should be given for interpreting Scripture in more practical situations such as preaching or pastoral care.

Some of this debate centers around the complaint often voiced that too many churches and denominations have given up on the ideal of a learned clergy, that is, a clergy educated in the biblical languages and classical disciplines of scholarly exegesis, history, and theology. Margaret Mitchell, of the University of Chicago Divinity School, feared the replacement of the ideal of a learned clergy by the therapeutic clergy. She argued that theological education must include a solid education in the history and thought of the student's own tradition, training in political action and how to go about it, and an emphasis on study as spiritual practice (to counter cultural and even ecclesiastical anti-intellectualism). My interviews suggest that the long-lived debate about how much of theological education should be oriented toward the traditional academic subjects and how much to training church workers in practical skills is not going away any time soon.

One thing almost all scholars I interviewed agreed on was the need for more interdisciplinary teaching. Several professors wished they had more opportunities for team-teaching with scholars of different specialties. Institutions sometimes make team-teaching difficult because they do not always allow both professors in a team-taught course to count that course toward the number of courses per semester or year they are required to teach. Team-teaching in some institutions, therefore, is (perhaps unintentionally) discouraged because it is seen as expensive and demanding more of the limited supply of teaching hours. Moreover, for many professors team-teaching is hard work, requiring sometimes even more preparation time working with other instructors to make the course experience truly valuable. Yet, although institutional and sometimes personal contraints mitigate against interdisciplinary and team-taught courses, professors I interviewed believed students would benefit from more such experiences.

A few professors fantasized about more radical changes in seminary organization. Stan Saunders, at Columbia Theological Seminary, for example, said that he would like to take the seminary out of seminary curriculum. He believes we should be training not professional clergy, but congregations. If he had his way, he said, he would take theological education out of the seminary confines and into the streets and congregations. Similarly, Phillis Shepherd, at North Park Theological Seminary, when asked whether she had an alternative fantasy curriculum, said, "Yes. Total fantasy: I would have Scripture read in groups and not just here at the seminary. For community justice and pastoral care, the sites we visit, I'd ask that people there read Scripture, and we talk about it in that context. What are the moral and ethical imperatives that arise out of reading Scripture in that context?"

Luke Timothy Johnson, at Emory University's Candler School of Theology, said he would organize the institution differently, moving away from the modern research university model of different disciplines, and back toward the social form of a collegium, a religious community. "I'd prefer to build the building differently. Have public spaces and public debates on issues by our best thinkers. I'd organize the curriculum more around topics and texts and questions that all of us could participate in discussing rather than different fields. . . . The oddity of the theology school is that it looks like a monastery but has no coherent practices the divine office provided." Steven Kraftchick, also at Candler, said something similar, suggesting that a curriculum could be organized each year around a particular topic (theological or ethical), with all subjects approached through the lens of that topic pursued by all the students and faculty. Another Candler professor, theologian Lewis Ayers, argued that the usual practice of exposing students to biblical studies first (often with Introduction to Hebrew Bible taught before New Testament studies) and then to theology should be changed. He argued that students should first be taught basic theological and critical thinking, then taught New Testament studies and history of interpretation, and only then taught critical study of the Old Testament. The basic motivation of all these ideas is a felt need to approach biblical studies more theologically, with the needs of the church and the history of Christian interpretation more fully in view.

As my brief and few surveys have shown, although some faculty are basically content with the current curricular arrangements of their institutions or would suggest only relatively minor changes, many recognize a need for a more integrated curriculum, including especially the need to address theological and ecclesiastical interpretations of Scripture. Among the scholars I interviewed, there is a general interest in preserving the expertise of the different guilds but not allowing those disciplinary boundaries and requirements to obscure the properly Christian reading of Scripture in community.

I asked professors to ignore realistic limitations and to fantasize about possible alternative curricular organizations. I found most professors not very well prepared for such unfettered fantasy. We all still tend to reproduce the pedagogical structures and practices with which we are familiar. But in this chapter, I attempt, at least to some extent, to ignore institutional constraints and contingencies—whether of the seminary structures themselves or the stated expectations and demands of denominations—and attempt freer imagination: an "ironic utopia." I borrow the term from David Kelsey. At the beginning of one of his books on theological education, he quotes a comment by Edward Farley, another scholar who has published much on theological education. According to Kelsey, "Edward Farley once ruefully observed that any essay on the nature and purposes of theological education is inescapably a contribution to utopian literature."[1] Yet sometimes it is fruitful to allow our imaginations to construct utopias and ideals. This chapter constitutes just such an attempt at "ironic utopia."

I feel the need also for an apologia. I know I'm going to get into trouble by publishing this chapter. There are bound to be essential points that I will not make; different scholars may feel that I am neglecting central subjects; and my unabashed suggestion, which I make below, that Scripture be put in the center of theological education may appear self-serving, since I am a scholar of Scripture myself. But I begin by admitting that this chapter represents only one possible view, an admittedly utopian one, and one offered with a sense of irony—precisely because I recognize that I myself do not teach in a theological school. In spite of my inadequacies, I feel that I must put some specific flesh on these theoretical bones. I mean this chapter as tentative and suggestive, not prescriptive—and certainly not confidently prescriptive. What follows is offered with fear and trepidation, and with respect for those who will inevitably disagree.

SCRIPTURE-CENTERED CURRICULUM

In the modern world, theological education, as has been repeatedly pointed out, became professionalized and organized to reflect the disciplinary structures of scholarship and the modern university. What I mean by "professionalized" is that theological schools increasingly saw themselves as training future leaders of churches in various skills believed necessary for serving as the professional manager of a congregation.[2] This approach meant including in theological education not only training in Scripture and theology, but also training in preaching and public speaking, denominational polity, and skills in organization and management. Consequently, the centrality of Scripture that had played an important role in premodern theological education came to be de-emphasized, and biblical studies became simply one part, though admittedly an important part, of the curriculum.

That curriculum, moreover, came to be divided into several disciplines, each of which structured itself according to the expectations of doctoral programs in the different subject areas and different guilds of scholars practicing in those subject areas. Biblical studies became divided into New Testament studies and Old Testament (or, reflecting an even greater degree of "de-Christianization" appropriate for a modern, secular, academic discipline, "Hebrew Bible"). Biblical scholars were no longer automatically seen to be theologians, and theologians were no longer expected to be experts in the scholarly exegesis of the Bible. Church historians were often educated not even in seminary doctoral programs or departments of religious studies, but in doctoral programs in history departments. As each of these different subject areas modeled themselves on scholarly disciplines, the subject areas themselves increasingly came to resemble not just subject areas, but academic disciplines in themselves. And since each of these disciplines came to occupy discrete parts of the theological curriculum, the previous centrality of Scripture gave way to a plurality of disciplines, of which biblical studies was one.

It may indeed come as something of a surprise to modern Christians, especially Protestants, that the study and interpretation of Scripture was central in premodern theological education. After all, Protestants often tell themselves that it was the Reformation that "reformed" the church by, for one thing, insisting that Scripture occupy the privileged role, if not the only role (*sola scriptura*), as authoritative source. But many scholars have recently emphasized that patristic and medieval theological education was centered, more than anywhere else, on the interpretation of Scripture. R. W. Southern argues as follows:

> The fundamental teaching method of the medieval schools, which they handed on to the universities that grew out of them, was the exposition

of authoritative texts. And of all the texts expounded in the schools there was none that could claim anything like the degree of authority and range of influence possessed by the Bible. It is necessary to begin by saying this, because one of the most widely held and longest lasting misconceptions about scholastic thought, which has lasted from the sixteenth century—and even earlier—almost to the present day, has been that it diminished the role of the Bible in the totality of Christian thought.[3]

And as Jean Leclercq insists, the centrality of Scripture was not invented by the medieval schools, but was something they inherited from patristic practices. Medieval practices "must be understood from the point of view of what preceded them—the patristic tradition whose principal task was to transmit and explain the Bible."[4]

One of the reasons, therefore, I urge that we reclaim the premodern heritage of centering theological education around Scripture is precisely because that would better connect us to the longer history and tradition of the church. Not only do we "have a lot to learn" from our premodern Christian forebears, but any concern for our own orthodoxy should bring with it a concern for connection with Christians of the past. We better enter into a living communion of the saints by learning from their examples.

Another reason I urge seminary education to place Scripture again at the center of the curriculum is because by doing so we may be better able to break out of the captivity of Scripture to modernity and historical criticism. The discipline of biblical studies is defined by, more than any other method, the scholarly and academic expectations of modern historical criticism. By putting the interpretation of Scripture again at the center of the curriculum, we take it out of the exclusive control of the specialists or experts of biblical studies. We move away from allowing the biblical faculty any role as gatekeepers of the Bible.

Thus it should now be clear that my suggestion that we make Scripture the center of theological education does not constitute, contrary to possible first impressions, the privileging of biblical studies or the faculty of Bible in the curriculum. Precisely because the professional theologians on the faculty may have quite different approaches to Scripture, and yet they will be expected to focus their pedagogy at least to a significant extent on Scripture, those theologians will not at all be marginalized by this curricular revision. When professional church historians focus on Scripture, as they teach about different historical movements, periods, or figures in history, what they have to offer about the study of Scripture will differ significantly from what a biblical scholar would say. Putting Scripture back in the center of theological education actually (ironically?) would de-emphasize any ownership of the study of the Bible sometimes expected of—or by—biblical scholars.

As emphasized in chapter 3, one of the important things we may learn from premodern Christians is how they read Scripture. Augustine, as illustrated already, prayed Scripture, but in a dialogical sense of prayer. He did appropriate its voice as his own, yet he also heard in its text the voice of God speaking directly to him. Simply the constancy with which many monks recited, sang, and heard Scripture meant that the words, stories, and images of Scripture came to saturate their environments and their bodies. In the early fifth century, for instance, Cassian quotes an abbot as insisting that Scripture "ought to be constantly poured into our ears or should ever proceed from our lips . . . And so it will come to pass that not only every purpose and thought of your heart, but also the wanderings and rovings of your imagination will become to you a holy and unceasing pondering of the Divine Law."[5] As Rowan Greer explains, "What he means, of course, is that Scripture will so purify the memory that the moral and spiritual life will be rightly directed. Cassian is thinking of the monastic offices and of the monk's constant prayers, which drew largely upon the treasures of Scripture."[6]

Douglas Burton-Christie points as well to the desert fathers of fourth-century Egypt, who, even if they lived alone or with only one other brother, and even if they were illiterate, came together regularly to hear Scripture read. Great emphasis was placed on reciting Scripture or singing psalms alone or with one or two brothers, before sleep and after sleep, during the night and all through the day. In the words of Burton-Christie, "The point of reciting the Scriptures was to become absorbed in the world of the texts, and desert fathers worked at this assiduously."[7] For these monastics, the interpretation of Scripture was never far from the very practice, living, and enacting of Scripture throughout the day.

R. W. Southern, speaking here in particular of Rupert of Deutz (ca. 1075–ca. 1117), describes the way medieval liturgies allowed Christians to become absorbed in the stories and narratives of Scripture so that, as they participated in the liturgy, they came to incorporate Scripture and be incorporated within it:

> As in the ceremonies of Palm Sunday every incident of the day was a drama, but much more than a drama: in a drama the actor assumes only for a moment the *persona* that he temporarily embodies; but, in the monastic day, these symbolic activities brought an intense experience of the supreme world-embracing reality in which the monastic community lived. Every item in the daily routine of the monastery was a declaration of the presence of God and of the whole company of heaven: it was theology in action. To take part in these actions and rituals, and to handle the symbolic objects, was to live through the historical process of redemption; it was to live in time, and yet to transcend time in a perpetual re-enactment of the greatest event

between Creation and the End of the world: the redemption of
mankind. This was prefigured in the details of the Exodus, propheti-
cally foreseen by the Prophets, actually accomplished in Christ, and
daily thereafter relived in the liturgy and in the ceremonies of the
monastic life.[8]

By living through the liturgy, the Christian enters the narrative world provided
by Scripture.

In holding up such premodern practices as possible models for modern
theological education, I realize that I may seem unrealistically ambitious. But
I do not expect that we could re-create a medieval world, nor would I want to
do so. I do urge, however, that we look to premodern practices of reading
Scripture, including placing Scripture in the center of theological education,
to help spark our own pedagogical imaginations for how we may teach the
interpretation of Scripture better in our own world.

One approach that has already found enthusiastic practioners in the past
several years, in schools and churches, is one also inspired by medieval monasticism: the practice of *lectio divina*. *Lectio divina* literally means "divine reading," and in the ancient and medieval worlds it could refer to the sacred text
itself, to simply the reading of Scripture, or to particular ways of using Scripture in prayer or meditation. Lately, the term has been resurrected to refer to
a specific method of praying with Scripture that has been taught and learned
by Christians of several different denominations and communities. Though
lectio divina in this more particular sense of the term requires discipline and
exercise to perform consistently and fruitfully, it is a rather simple method to
teach—thus its popularity for populations of Christians seeking more spiritual
and meaningful encounters with Scripture.[9]

The renewed interest in *lectio divina* seems to have grown out of a renewed
interest in meditative prayer in Christian groups, usually associated with what
many have called "centering prayer." People are taught to read (*lectio*) a text,
but slowly and repeatedly. They are instructed to read but also to listen to
Scripture and God speaking in Scripture. Meditation (*meditatio*) on a word or
a passage follows. Then the person enters into prayer proper (*oratio*), understood not simply as talking to God, but as entering into dialogue with God,
perhaps also through the words of the text or with other words and images.
Finally, the session ends in contemplation (*contemplatio*), resting in silence in
the experience of love and the presence of God.

Lectio divina, therefore, more broadly refers to the entire way people may
live in and with Scripture, using the words of Scripture to express their own
feelings, needs, or experiences, and attempting to insert oneself within the
"world created by the text."[10] But more narrowly, it also refers to a rather simply communicated, easily taught method for learning to pray and meditate

through the words of Scripture. This teaching of the practice of *lectio divina* would be easy to incorporate into a seminary curriculum. I'm convinced that students would be better served if they were taught this practice of reading Scripture even before encountering the more technical method of historical criticism or other critical approaches to the Bible, as I explore further below.

All these suggestions and borrowings from premodern Christian notions and practices are meant to help us imagine Scripture differently, to imagine what sort of thing Scripture is, and therefrom to imagine Christian ways of reading and interpreting Scripture that move beyond modernist methods. In the previous chapter, I suggested that I have been helped by thinking of Scripture as sacred space we may enter, rather than merely as a linear text we read. Elsewhere, I have imagined Scripture as a cathedral that we may enter, roam around in, and from which we may derive all sorts of information and inspiration through multiple ways of seeing, hearing, and experiencing. I have offered these accounts of premodern use of Scripture to demonstrate that placing Scripture in the center of a theological curriculum need not imply any hegemony over the interpretation and use of Scripture by the modernist guild of biblical studies and historical criticism. Indeed, placing Scripture once again in the center may lead to new—or renewed—ways of interpreting and living with and in Scripture. In the following sections, I move to more specific proposals for curricular revision and reform.

KEY ASSUMPTIONS AND GOALS

Before offering specific curricular suggestions, I should make clear certain assumptions with which I begin in thinking about biblical studies in theological education and what goals I have in mind. The reader may think of these as principles that motivate and inform my proposals.

Teach historical criticism, but as one among other ways of reading. I am myself a historical critic of the New Testament and a historian of early Christianity. Like many other scholars, I believe historical criticism has in many cases been a benefit to Christians. Students often enter theological school with ways of reading Scripture that are comfortable and self-serving. Churches often tame Scripture or ideologically construe its meaning so that it affirms rather than challenges their beliefs, prejudices, and even complicity with oppressive powers. In less ominous cases, students simply read Scripture so that it teaches rather innocuous but uninteresting platitudes and easy pieties. The interpretations furnished by historical criticism, as many professors will attest, may serve as leverage to dislodge harmful or simply boring appropriations of Scripture, hasty accommodations of the text to our own culture. The historical-critical method, as described in chapter 1, is not a particularly easy method to master. Teaching it requires time and energy, but the potential benefits of historical criticism are worth the investment. I therefore believe that in the current climate we should continue to teach theological students historical criticism of the Bible. But I urge that we teach it as one way of reading among several others, and not as a privileged way of reading—especially not as the privileged way of reading.

Retain the expertise of different disciplinary scholarship and scholars, but integrate the different disciplines and use them in conjunction with one another. Again, I am not urging schools to dispense with the specific knowledges, skills, and practices embodied in the now-traditional disciplines of theological education, such as biblical studies, systematic theology, history, ethics, philosophy, and so forth. The pursuit of excellence in education demands that the criteria of excellence that serve as standards in the respective academic guilds be respected. For example, if schools are to teach students the history of the Christian church, as I believe they should, those teaching that history should be properly trained historians who understand and can practice modern historiography. I urge, therefore, not that schools dispense with the disciplines but that they be combined and integrated much better than they are now. Moreover, they should be used in conjunction with one another, not in isolation and certainly not in competition.

Teach theology of Scripture before teaching different methods of interpreting Scripture. In many schools, the curriculum is organized so that students are taught Bible early in the curriculum, with systematic theology to follow. The idea that students are regularly given, though often not intentionally, is that the Bible functions or ought to function as foundational information or data, and that other subjects, such as theology or ethics, are seen as the application of truths seen first in Scripture. The idea one often encounters among students is that they first must learn what it meant before they can consider what it means for us. I believe this is a confusing way to teach biblical studies if the eventual goal is the theological use of the Bible as Scripture. In my view, students should be taught to think about what Scripture is in a Christian context before they are introduced to the practices of historical criticism or any other method of reading. They should be led through discoveries of different theologies of Scripture so that they will have proper contexts in which to understand why they are reading Scripture in the first place and how they should think about reading Scripture Christianly. In order for the historical reading of the text or any other method of reading to make sense in a Christian context, the very nature of Scripture and proper Christian ways of thinking about Scripture and its interpretation must be considered. Otherwise, students have no good theological understanding of why they are being taught the particular method they are learning.

Teach theology first by teaching theological thinking and interpretation. Teach systematic theology later, as a more advanced subject. The suggestions in the previous paragraph should not be taken to mean that students must be led through a full course in systematic theology before learning methods of exegesis. It just means that they should be exposed to critical theological thinking about what Scripture is and how Christians think about Scripture theologically before learning biblical interpretation itself. In fact, I think that introducing students to theological thinking at different stages is a good idea. Since systematic theology regularly turns to Scripture and its interpretation, students need knowledge of Scripture to learn and evaluate different theological systems. But that simply means that the aspects of theology students should be taught before encountering critical study of the Bible should be those that relate to Christian notions about the Bible first. More advanced study of theology and philosophy may come later.

Early in the educational process, introduce theories of interpretation, literary theory, and philosophies of interpretation and textuality. In my surveys and discussions with students in theological schools, one discovery impressed itself on me perhaps more than any other: students who will be spending the rest of their lives, quite possibly, interpreting texts seem consistently to be relatively ignorant about theories of textuality and interpretation. They have simplistic and naïve notions about what a text is and what different possibilities exist for interpretation. They cannot really articulate even quite traditional literary theories, much less enter into a discussion of the debates in critical theory about interpretation of the past thirty years or so. Though I am not saying that students must become experts in philosophical hermeneutics or that they must spend their lives in such intellectual pursuits, I am arguing that students should be taught some basic ways of thinking critically about issues of textuality, meaning, and interpretation, and this exposure should come early in the students' school experience.

Include and integrate artistic, literary, and musical interpretations of Scripture. This is a proposal with which almost everyone I interviewed agreed, even as they bemoaned how difficult it is to do. Repeatedly, I have found that biblical scholars, not to mention experts in other subjects, recognize how fruitful it can be to become familiar with scriptural quotation and allusion in art, literature, and music. Our world is not, and has never been, one captured or expressed completely in the linearity of linguistic texts. We are surrounded by visual stimulation and musical communication. Even for those people who do not make a habit of reading much fiction, story surrounds us all. An appreciation for what can be learned about and from Scripture as mediated in art, literature, and music is easy and obvious. The regular reason given by educators for not including such materials more in formal schooling is a dearth of time, expertise, or resources. I argue that schools must consciously and energetically insert such materials and training about them in theological education. To do less is to miss great opportunities for communicating the gospel—and for enlivening the imagination about Scripture and its interpretation.

Introduce practical disciplines all along the way, perhaps concentrating on them toward the end. I have given little attention to the teaching of those theological disciplines often grouped under practical theology, such as preaching, pastoral care, church organization and management, and so forth. This lack should not be taken to mean that I find those subjects irrelevant or unimportant. It rather reflects the fact that I have little to recommend. If I am an amateur in the subject of theological education, I am even less knowledgeable about the aspects of ministry we might call practical. I am convinced, though, that skills must be learned from these subjects. I tend to think that these skills and issues should be raised consistently all through theological education. Issues often encountered in situations of pastoral counseling may be brought out within a context of biblical interpretation. Questions about preaching may be raised whenever Scripture is encountered. I think it makes sense, however, for concentrated courses in practical disciplines to be grouped toward the end of the curricular career, closer to the time when students will be entering full-time ministerial positions.

With these principles made explicit, let us imagine more specifically how a seminary and its curriculum might be structured.

A MAYPOLE CURRICULUM

In my fantasy seminary, the different disciplines delineated and elaborated by modern educational institutions would not be done away with, but they would be better integrated and related to one another. The image that comes to mind for me is one of a maypole with several differently colored ribbons. Modern biblical criticism of the Old Testament and the New Testament are two ribbons. They may, of course, be thought of as one, but today most scholars are trained as scholars of either the Hebrew Bible or the New Testament, and in many aspects their training is methodologically somewhat different. Systematic theology, the history of Christianity, homiletics, pastoral care, Christian education, ethics, philosophy of religion, and any other separately delineated discipline we could agree on are each ribbons. Rather than keeping each discipline in its own box, or even setting them side by side occasionally, a seminary education should consist of choreography among many participants that weaves the ribbons in and around one another to form, eventually, an education that is a woven, tapestrylike pattern of colored ribbons. The different disciplines have not disappeared; they have just become much more consciously and elaborately mingled with one another, and without an insidious hierarchy among them being retained.

In my fantasy seminary, students would learn together in community by living either together or in close proximity. The institution would resemble a medieval monastic community more than a modern school in its combination of common life, regular worship and liturgy, and shared learning. The use of Scripture in worship would precede the critical study of it. Theological study of what Scripture "is" or should be, along with the historical and critical study of theology of Scripture, would come between the liturgical encounter of Scripture and the later learning of critical methods of interpreting Scripture. At least some aspects of philosophical hermeneutics and contemporary and postmodern theories of textuality and interpretation would also be taught early on in the curriculum.

My seminary would certainly include training in modern historical-critical methods, along with the discovery of how such methods may distance the text from prior Christian experience of the Bible. The benefits of historical criticism would be made explicit, but historical criticism would be placed in the curriculum as one among several other ways of reading the text: ancient and medieval, allegorical and anagogical, literary readings, feminist and postcolonial interpretations, African American, Latino/a, and other liberationist and identity-perspective approaches to biblical study.

The further learning of historical and systematic theology would be encountered by centering on readings of Scripture, much as medieval theology was considered commentary on Scripture. The history of Christianity, and possibly also the history and practices of other religions, would also be taught alongside notions and practices of scriptural interpretation. Preaching, pastoral care, and the other traditionally considered practical disciplines would be encountered and engaged regularly within the study of Scripture and the other academic disciplines.

This sort of curriculum would not deny the importance of having experts representing the different guilds of modern scholarship, but it would require much cooperation among the faculty, team-teaching, and mingling of disciplinary interests among the faculty.

I have thus proposed some bare ideas of what seminary would look like constructed along the lines of a premodern religious community. I admit that to construct a seminary along these lines would require a radical departure from most current practices. I nonetheless think the experiment would be worthwhile. I would also insist, however, that many of my suggestions could be incorporated even in existing institutions of theological education. We might think, for example, of retaining current institutional forms—for example, a three-year master of divinity program of six semesters and four courses each semester, with some core requirements supplemented by electives—and still go a long way toward implementing my recommendations. Let me offer one such imagination of a sequence of core course requirements.

THREE UNITS OF FOUR

I here offer one way of imagining a curriculum centered around Scripture, teaching different methods of biblical interpretation, including historical criticism, and incorporating other important aspects of theological education. I organize it in three different units of four courses each. These may be thought about as three separate semesters, which would constitute the first three out of six semesters of a seminary program. Or they could be thought of as each constituting the first semester of each of three years, with the second semester of each year made up of electives or further study in any area needed. One could even split each unit of four into six units of two courses, requiring students to take two of these courses each semester and supplementing them with two other courses each semester. The important thing is that some of the basic sequencing should be retained (introduction to theology of Scripture before or at least at the same time as introduction to historical criticism; theory of interpretation encountered early on, and so forth), and that the basic principles and goals outlined above should inform the organization. The units are here designated by roman numerals, and separate courses by letters.

I. Year/Semester 1
  A. Theology of Scripture, a course that would include:
    1. Reading the central, early creeds and reflecting on basic, traditional doctrines of the church. This is relevant not only for the more creedal churches, but also for those that do not explicitly found themselves on or concentrate on the creeds. Almost all Christian denominations are heavily influenced by the creeds even if they don't realize it.[11]
    2. Teaching students to reflect on their own beliefs and traditions about Scripture: what implicit or explicit models of Scripture have they imbibed in their churches or the culture more generally? What are their own assumptions about what Scripture is?
    3. Thinking critically about how we want to think about what Scripture is. Construct and defend Christian models of Scripture.
  B. Historical Criticism of the Hebrew Bible/Old Testament
    An introduction to the text of the OT, some history of the period, and historical methods for its study. This should be primarily an introduction to method rather than a full survey of all the content of the OT.

C. The Old Testament in Christian Interpretation
A survey of how Christians have read the OT, beginning with New Testament authors, and moving to patristic, medieval, and modern examples. Focus on different theological interpretations (including good and problematic ideological readings) of the OT from antiquity to the present. Some art and literature may be used also, though more explicit courses on those will come later in the curriculum. This course will also function as a brief, summary introduction to church history, which will also be more fully explored later.

D. Theories of Text and Interpretation
Students will be introduced to theories of textuality and interpretation, twentieth-century literary theory, and philosophy of interpretation. They will be taught to think about and discuss questions such as: What is a text? What is meaning? Where is it located? How does one approach the ethics of interpretation? Other ways of reading the Bible will be learned (literary criticism, ideological criticism, and so forth).

II. Year/Semester 2
A. Historical Introduction to the New Testament and Early Christianity
A historical introduction to the history of the NT, Christianity in the first two centuries, some Second Temple Judaism, and methods of historical criticism of the NT. This might indeed look much like a current, traditional Introduction to the New Testament course, concentrating on historical criticism and the ancient context and meaning of the NT.

B. Patristic and Early Christian Literature and Interpretation of the Bible
This course would introduce students to the Christianity and culture of late antiquity, concentrating on the interpretation of Scripture, but including other issues of culture and theology. Patristic theology itself, with its particular interests, would be included but may be approached by seeing how the fathers and other early Christian writers interpret Scripture in their theological writings and debates.

C. Medieval and Early Modern Christianity and Biblical Interpretation
Same as the above course on early Christianity, but with concentration on the medieval and early modern period.

D. The Bible in Visual Art, Literature, and Music

III. Year/Semester 3
A. Medieval and Modern Theologians
This course would constitute an introduction to systematic theologies and theologians.

B. Scripture in Liturgy and Preaching

C. Scripture in World: Christian Scripture in comparison with other religions and their use of authoritative texts. This course should include, if it is not covered elsewhere in the curriculum, exposure also to post-colonial interpretations and notions of Scripture—that is, the diverse ways peoples of other cultures in the world may read Scripture differently from people in Europe and North America.

D. Pastoral Counseling and Congregational Life

This curricular recommendation is much less radical than my fantasy presented earlier of reorganizing the entire life and structure of a seminary, but its merits are that it could be incorporated into the structure of many current theological schools. It is an attempt to maintain the virtues of the modern disciplines of theological education but to integrate them better and to stress the importance of theological and liturgical interpretation of Scripture. An added benefit of this more modest recommendation is that it provides more flexibility for different institutional and individual modification or addition to this core curriculum. Those students, for example, wanting to take Hebrew and Greek or other languages during their seminary time could be allowed to substitute a language course for one of these core required courses, with the stipulation that they would take the core course in a later semester. Or the core courses could be spread out over more semesters, thereby freeing up course time in each semester for language work.

The main goal, in any case, should be kept in mind as much as possible: to institute integration of biblical studies with theology, church history, the study of other interpretations of Scripture (e.g., art, literature, music), and exposure to theory of interpretation; and to expose students to theologies of Scripture before or at the same time as introducing them to historical criticism of the Bible.

Learning to interpret Scripture Christianly is like learning to improvise in music or acting. Others have suggested that it is like learning to play a game. Games do not prescribe exact behavior or movements. They set up rules within which players have a considerable amount of freedom. A particular play will not necessarily lead to success. Certain movements and behaviors are excluded. There are boundaries. Learning to play a game well means learning the rules and normal movements required by the game—even incorporating them so that they become second nature or habit. Players who play a game well are those who, on the one hand, develop habits of moving and thinking that remain within the boundaries of the rules of the game, but who, on the other hand, use those rules and normal movements creatively to attain the desired goals of the game.

Interpreting Scripture is like that. Theological education should teach and develop the habits and skills appropriate for the Christian interpretation of Scripture.

CONCLUSION

My purpose in this chapter—and throughout this book—has been to open discussion and dialogue, not to set myself up as an expert. Though I may pass as an expert in New Testament studies, I could never pass as an expert either on education in general or theological education in particular. But as I noted in the preface, I am a scholar and a churchperson with personal interests in the education of both leaders of churches and members of churches, as well as in changing the way people in American culture more broadly think about the Bible and its interpretation. I have come to believe that at least one place to begin such a change is with our formal institutions of theological education.

The exercise and expanding of the Christian imagination is never ending, and I am under no delusion that what I offer here is a solution. My intention with publishing this book is to enter a discussion that has already been going on for a long time. If I have anything to contribute, I believe it is precisely because I am a scholar of the New Testament who has published studies of the Bible that are firmly at home within the modern—and in some cases postmodern—study of the Bible. As a historical critic, I am insisting that we must put aside the modern hegemony of historical criticism; that historical criticism cannot provide the Christian meaning of the text; that we do ourselves, our churches, and our students a disservice by allowing historical criticism the domination it currently enjoys in theological education. We must radically rethink what it means to teach theological, Christian practices of reading and performing Scripture. We must ourselves learn how to teach the living of Scripture.

Notes

Chapter 1

1. For one good introduction to the rise of modern biblical scholarship and historical criticism, as well as the contemporary scene (though with here an emphasis on Old Testament studies), see Walter Brueggemann, *Theology of the Old Testament: Testimony, Dispute, Advocacy* (Minneapolis: Fortress, 1997), 1–114.

2. The point is made explicitly by some authors in a collection of essays, and seems to be assumed by just about all of them: Elmer Dyck, ed., *The Act of Bible Reading: A Multidisciplinary Approach to Biblical Interpretation* (Downers Grove, IL: InterVarsity, 1996). Gordon D. Fee, for example, insists that "exegesis" is "the determination of the originally intended meaning of a text." See his contribution to the collection, "History as Context for Interpretation," at 11. But this assumption is made by many biblical scholars, of many different theological tendencies.

3. Several books survey and explain different methods currently used in studying Scripture. See, for example, Steven L. McKenzie and Stephen R. Haynes, eds., *To Each Its Own Meaning: An Introduction to Biblical Criticisms and Their Application*, rev. and expanded (Louisville, KY: Westminster John Knox, 1999); see also Mark Roncace and Patrick Gray, *Teaching the Bible: Practical Strategies for Classroom Instruction* (Leiden and Boston: Brill, 2005).

4. Several important studies of modern theological education describe the historical process that led to current disciplinary structures of theological education, and critique those structures. See especially Edward Farley, *Theologia: The Fragmentation and Unity of Theological Education* (Philadelphia: Fortress, 1983), esp. 4–10 (though Farley argues that the different "areas of study" are not properly "disciplines"); Farley, *The Fragility of Knowledge: Theological Education in the Church and the University* (Philadelphia: Fortress, 1988), esp. 126; David H. Kelsey, *To Understand God Truly: What's Theological about a Theological School* (Louisville, KY: Westminster/John Knox, 1992), esp. 86–87.

5. For further studies of theological education, besides those by Farley and Kelsey mentioned above, see Jackson W. Carroll, Barbara G. Wheeler, Daniel O. Aleshire, and Penny Long Marler, *Being There: Culture and Formation in Two Theological Schools* (New York and Oxford: Oxford University Press, 1997), which intriguingly provides an in-depth study of just two seminaries, one "evangelical" and the other more "mainstream" or "liberal." See also Charles R. Foster, Lisa E. Dahill, Lawrence A. Golemon, and Barbara Wang Tolentino, *Educating Clergy: Teaching Practices and Pastoral Imagination* (San Francisco: Jossey-Bass, 2006); and for earlier studies: Joseph C. Hough and John B. Cobb,

Christian Identity and Theological Education (Atlanta: Scholars Press, 1985); Charles M. Wood, *Vision and Discernment: An Orientation in Theological Study* (Atlanta: Scholars Press, 1985); The Mudflower Collective, *God's Fierce Whimsy: Christian Feminism and Theological Education* (New York: Pilgrim, 1985).

Chapter 2

1. Much of this discussion, along with much of my argument in this chapter, may be found in a different form in my *Sex and the Single Savior: Gender and Sexuality in Biblical Interpretation* (Louisville, KY: Westminster John Knox, 2006), esp. chaps. 1 and 11.

2. Stanley Fish, *Is There a Text in This Class? The Authority of Interpretive Communities* (Cambridge, MA: Harvard University Press, 1980), 322. For astute uses of and dialogues with Fish's ideas from a New Testament scholar, see A. K. M. Adam, *Faithful Interpretation: Reading the Bible in a Postmodern World* (Minneapolis: Fortress, 2006), passim, but see esp. 125–30.

3. Fish, *Is There a Text in This Class?* 326.

4. Jonathan Culler, "Making Sense," *Twentieth-Century Studies* 12 (1974): 27–36, at 29.

5. "For example, the signifier STOP on a traffic sign is not susceptible of infinitely various construals" (Richard B. Hays, *The Moral Vision of the New Testament: Community, Cross, New Creation: A Contemporary Introduction to New Testament Ethics* [San Francisco: HarperSanFrancisco, 1996], 11n24). Hays does not explain, though, how he knows where to draw the limiting line that would forever close off other possible interpretations, or where that line in fact is. In the same note, Hays claims, "Apart from the assumption that texts have limited ranges of meaning, ordered social discourse would be impossible." This is, of course, false, as the observation of social discourse demonstrates. We have ordered social discourse as long as all of us doing the discoursing are playing by the same rules generally in interpreting the signs that matter for social order, as long as we assume the same things about the signs, their meaning, and proper interpretation. But that does not at all demonstrate that the signs simply contain in themselves the meaning ready to be passively observed by different readers. Common socialization of interpreters means that interpreters in a given society will tend to interpret similarly, so that public discourse can proceed in an orderly manner.

6. Besides *Is There a Text in This Class?* already mentioned, see also Fish, *Doing What Comes Naturally: Change, Rhetoric, and the Practice of Theory in Literary and Legal Studies* (Durham, NC: Duke University Press, 1989), e.g., 26, 141–42, et passim.

7. A. K. M. Adam, *What Is Postmodern Biblical Criticism?* (Minneapolis: Fortress, 1995), 19.

8. See, for example, Kevin J. Vanhoozer, "The Reader in New Testament Interpretation," in *Hearing the New Testament: Strategies for Interpretation*, ed. Joel B. Green, 301–28 (Grand Rapids: Wm. B. Eerdmans, 1995), 316.

9. Portions of Ps. 22, King James Version. I have made a collage of verses and parts of verses, and the final words reflect not the KJV here but the interpretation of the psalm by early Christians.

10. In previous generations of scholarship, the claim that Christianity is a historical religion was made in order to differentiate Christian "truths" from the "myths" of ancient Greek and Roman religions, but as more recent scholarship

has shown, that was a specious claim advanced merely for apologetic purposes of making Christianity seem superior to other religions. See Jonathan Z. Smith, *Drudgery Divine: On the Comparison of Early Christianities and the Religions of Late Antiquity* (Chicago: Chicago University Press, 1990), esp. 105. For other criticisms of the claim that Christianity is a historical religion, see Maurice Wiles, *Maurice Wiles*, Explorations in Theology 4 (London: SCM, 1979), 53–65; James Barr, *The Scope and Authority of the Bible* (Philadelphia: Westminster, 1980), 6–17, 30–50; Frances Young, "Allegory and the Ethics of Reading," in *Open Text: New Dimensions for Biblical Studies?* ed. Francis Watson, 103–20 (London: SCM, 1993).

11. See Elizabeth A. Clark, *History, Theory, Text: Historians and the Linguistic Turn* (Cambridge, MA: Harvard University Press, 2004), 156, passim; Keith Jenkins, *Re-thinking History: With a New Preface and Conversation with the Author by Alun Munslow* (London: Routledge, 2003).

12. Though the claim has been either made explicitly or assumed by many, for one recent example see N. T. Wright, *The Last Word: Beyond the Bible Wars to a New Understanding of the Authority of Scripture* (San Francisco: HarperSanFrancisco, 2005), 67, 132–33, 109.

13. This has been generally true, though not universally and in all times. See James Samuel Preus, *From Shadow to Promise: Old Testament Interpretation from Augustine to the Young Luther* (Cambridge, MA: Harvard University Press, 1969); see also my *Sex and the Single Savior*, esp. 11–13.

14. Again, I want to be clear that I am not necessarily advocating that we Christians today must work with a notion of God's intention as containing the meaning of the text. I prefer most of the time to work with a notion simply of the text as space for the creation of meaning, without worrying about intentions at all. But the point I am here making is that when contemporary historians and theologians claim that Christians have always or typically, even in the premodern world, equated the literal sense with the intentions of the human author, they are mistaken.

Chapter 3

1. For patristic and Jewish interpretations, see James L. Kugel and Rowan A. Greer, *Early Biblical Interpretation*, Library of Early Christianity (Philadelphia: Westminster, 1986). An older, now classic, but still valuable history of medieval interpretation is Beryl Smalley, *The Study of the Bible in the Middle Ages*, 3rd ed., rev. (Oxford: Blackwell, 1983). For a more recent survey, in the form of essays on key ancient and medieval figures written by different scholars, see Justin S. Holcomb, ed., *Christian Theologies of Scripture: A Comparative Introduction* (New York: New York University Press, 2006). For a very valuable, recent study of the history of Anglican theology and interpretation of Scripture, see Rowan A. Greer, *Anglican Approaches to Scripture: From the Reformation to the Present* (New York: Crossroad, 2006).

2. I put "Christian" in quotation marks because it is inaccurate, of course, to call Jesus a Christian, and it is even anachronistic in many ways to use the term for many of the writers of the New Testament. Scholars of Paul's letters, for instance, increasingly recognize that Paul never used the term, thought of himself completely as a Jew, and did not think of his ministry as founding a new "religion." Paul may not have even known the term "Christian"; if he did, it may be significant that he never used it.

3. I provide fuller comments on these passages in *Sex and the Single Savior*, 133–34.
4. Again, my presentation here is abbreviated. I have discussed Paul's interpretation of Scripture more fully elsewhere (see *Sex and the Single Savior*, 151–56), but for a much more extensive and expert treatment, see Christopher D. Stanley, *Paul and the Language of Scripture: Citation Technique in the Pauline Epistles and Contemporary Literature* (Cambridge: Cambridge University Press, 1992), and Stanley, *Arguing with Scripture: The Rhetoric of Quotations in the Letters of Paul* (New York: T. & T. Clark, 2004).
5. See Joseph T. Lienhard, introduction to *Origen: Homilies on Luke; and, Fragments on Luke*, trans. Lienhard, The Fathers of the Church 94 (Washington, DC: Catholic University of America Press, 1996), xxi.
6. Ibid., xxii.
7. See, for example, Margaret M. Mitchell, "Patristic Rhetoric on Allegory: Origen and Eustathius Put 1 Samuel 28 on Trial," *The Journal of Religion* 85 (2005): 414–45.
8. Lienhard, introduction, xvi–xvii.
9. Ibid., 138. Words in parentheses are in the translation quoted. The explanation in square brackets is my addition.
10. I use the translation by Rowan A. Greer and Margaret M. Mitchell, *The "Belly-Myther" of Endor: Interpretations of 1 Kingdoms 28 in the Early Church* (Atlanta: Society of Biblical Literature, 2007), 32–61.
11. According to Greer and Mitchell, Origen is playing with two different meanings of "raising": Samuel was "elevated," and this last interpretation is of the more "elevated" meaning of the text. See ibid., 61n49.
12. The "flaming sword" is a reference to the closing of paradise narrated in Gen. 3:24. The sword kept humans from paradise from the time of Adam to the time of Christ, in Origen's interpretation.
13. A point Garry Wills makes about the text of the *Confessions* is also apropos as a description of how Augustine approached Scripture itself: "The text does not deliver us a product, but calls us into a process" (Wills, *Saint Augustine* [London: Orion House, 2000], 98).
14. I cite the translation by Maria Boulding. See Augustine, *The Confessions*, trans. Maria Boulding, preface by Patricia Hampl (New York: Vintage, 1998).
15. These translations of the psalms by Boulding are, of course, from the Latin, and from versions of the Latin that predate the Vulgate and were translations from the Greek Septuagint version of the psalms. They will not conform, therefore, to modern English translations, which are from scholarly reconstructions of the Hebrew.
16. See the fuller discussion of *lectio divina* in chap. 5 below and bibliography there cited for explanations of the practice, its history, and current revival.
17. See, for example, The Venerable Bede, *Commentary on the Acts of the Apostles*, trans. with an introduction and notes by Lawrence T. Martin (Kalamazoo, MI: Cistercian, 1989), 14, 23n6.
18. Ibid., 89; I cite the translation of Martin.
19. Ibid., 90.
20. See, for example, his interpretation of Acts 9:26; ibid., 89.
21. Ibid., 91. See 94n2 and 22n2 for explanations by Martin for this translation.
22. Ann W. Astell, *The Song of Songs in the Middle Ages* (Ithaca, NY: Cornell University Press, 1990), 19.

23. I use the translation found in Bernard of Clairvaux, *On the Song of Songs, Sermones super Cantica Canticorum*, trans. Kilian Walsh, introduction by Corneille Halfants, 4 vols. (Spencer, MA: Cistercian, 1971–1980).

24. The numbers of the psalms here correspond to those of the Latin Bible, not modern English editions. In most cases, one can find the reference in the English in the next psalm. Thus what is cited in Walsh's translation as Ps. 103:32 may be found at 104:32 in an English Bible.

25. See Thomas Aquinas, *Commentary on the Gospel of St. John*, trans. James A. Weisheipl with Fabian R. Larcher, Aquinas Scripture Series, vol. 4, pt. 1 (Albany, NY: Magi, 1980). For this section, see 281–88. I am grateful to my colleague Denys Turner for introducing me to the passage and for discussions about it.

26. Ibid., Lecture 1, 707 (p. 285).

27. Peter M. Candler Jr. ("St. Thomas Aquinas," in Holcomb, ed., *Christian Theologies of Scripture*, 60–80, at 67, 68) insightfully describes Thomas's use of Scripture: "Thomas's language regarding Holy Scripture often possesses this sense of motion about it; scripture is never a static deposit of propositional truth to which one can refer as if there were a simple meaning to be found therein, one that corresponded univocally to a reality that had only to be 'read.'" And unlike many modernist (Christian!) notions, the reading of Scripture for Thomas cannot be separated out from "tradition": "There is no pure, undefiled, 'original' deposit of teaching, even in the scriptures themselves, that is not already mediated and already a 'tradition.' In other words, one who teaches divine wisdom is handing over what one has already received. The teaching *is* the passing on—an activity already present in scripture itself. Thus, for Thomas scripture is not a 'source' in the modern sense, much less a 'book,' but a teaching, an activity, a *doctrina*, that cannot be understood except as a *traditio*—a handing over of and a being handed over to the constantly repeated truth of God, which is nowhere isolable nor possessible in an atomistic fashion, but is nevertheless one in its eternal simplicity. This unity is, however, disclosed in a multiplicity of signs, no single one of which is adequate to 'contain' the truth."

28. Note how Lesley Smith describes the views of Peter Comestor (died ca. 1178): "Comestor says scripture provides the foundation, walls, and roof of the dining room in which we eat and drink the stuff of eternal life." See Lesley Smith, "The Use of Scripture in Teaching at the Medieval University," in *Learning Institutionalized: Teaching in the Medieval University*, ed. John van Engen, 229–243 (Notre Dame, IN: University of Notre Dame Press, 2000), 239. To cite another premodern spatial image: that evoked by Aelred of Rievaulx (1109–1167) of Scripture as a "field" merits a long quotation. "This field, as it seems to me, is holy scripture, a fertile field indeed, full of every blessing. 'Behold,' he says, 'the smell of my son is as the smell of a plentiful field which the Lord hath blessed.' In this field there is the smell of myrrh and incense and every spice of the perfumer. Truly, brethren, there is no virtue, no insight, no wisdom whose smell is not fragrant in this field. And who is full of every blessing, full of every scent of this field, this plentiful field which the Lord hath blessed? Consider. In none of the saints can the fulness of every virtue be found. In David the virtue of humility is specially praised; in Job one detects the smell of patience with a stronger sweetness. Joseph is chaste, Moses is meek, Joshua is strong, Solomon is wise. Yet of none of these can it be said that his smell is

like the smell of a plentiful field. In truth the smell of my dearest Lord Jesus is above every perfume, his smell is like the smell of a plentiful field which the Lord hath blessed. Whatever wisdom, whatever virtue, whatever grace is found in the sacred page will all be discovered in him, in whom all the fulness of the godhead dwells corporeally, in whom all the treasures of wisdom and knowledge lie hid, to whom God does not give the spirit by measure, of whose fulness we have all received." Quoted in Aelred Squire, *Aelred of Rievaulx: A Study* (Kalamazoo, MI: Cistercian, 1981), 66–67; from *Sermones inediti B. Aelredi Abbatis Rievallensis*, ed. C. H. Talbot, Series scriptorum S. Ordinis Cisterciensis 1 (Rome: Curiam Generalem Sacri Ordinis Cisterciensis, 1952), 73–74.

Chapter 4

1. The term "the Yale theology" has been used to refer to a conjunction of certain themes in Christian theology that one could argue coalesced around the teachings and writings of, primarily, three theologians working at Yale in the 1970s and 1980s: Hans W. Frei, George A. Lindbeck, and David H. Kelsey. Frei's work emphasized the importance of narrative for understanding the meaning of Scripture, best represented in his two most famous books, *The Eclipse of Biblical Narrative: A Study in Eighteenth- and Nineteenth-Century Hermeneutics* (New Haven, CT: Yale University Press, 1974); and *The Identity of Jesus Christ: The Hermeneutical Bases of Dogmatic Theology* (Philadelphia: Fortress, 1975). Lindbeck, in his book *The Nature of Doctrine: Religion and Theology in a Postliberal Age* (Philadelphia: Westminster, 1984), proposed a new model for thinking about what sort of thing Christian doctrine is. He suggested that rather than thinking of Christian statements as either propositions whose truth lies in the accuracy of their correspondence to external reality, or as expressions of human religious "experience," we should think about Christian doctrine as the grammar of a social-linguistic system whose meaningfulness derives from internal structures and intratextuality. David Kelsey became well-known around the same time for studies of how different theologians and communities read and use Scripture, arguing that we must pay attention not only to what people say about Scripture, but also how Scripture actually functions for scholars and faith communities. His most famous book on this topic is *The Uses of Scripture in Recent Theology* (Philadelphia: Fortress, 1985), revised and republished as *Proving Doctrine: The Uses of Scripture in Modern Theology* (Harrisburg, PA: Trinity Press International, 1999). This combination of narrative theology, the theory of religions as sociolinguistic systems, and the centrality of Scripture characterizes key aspects of what people have often meant by the term "the Yale theology."

2. Here, at the beginning of my discussion of what theology is, and therefore what should constitute theological education, I should explicitly admit my disagreement with some theologians who insist that theology or theological education is not about language or beliefs about God, but about God. Miroslav Volf, for example: "I take it that theology is not simply reflection about how communities of faith use language about God—not 'critical talk about talk about God.' God, not just human talk about God, is the proper object of theology" (Miroslav Volf, "Theology for a Way of Life," in *Practicing Theology: Beliefs and Practices in Christian Life*, ed. Miroslav Volf and Dorothy C. Bass, 245–63 [Grand Rapids: Eerdmans, 2002], 260). Or note the way David Kelsey says that the "end" or "goal" of theological study is "understanding of God" (*To Under-*

stand God Truly, 34, et passim). In one sense, I could agree that theology is talk about God or seeking to understand God. For example, one may mean by such claims that, for some people, doing theology is itself an act of faith. I object to Volf's and Kelsey's statements, though, because I think they mislead in at least two significant ways. First, such claims make it sound as if through our study we somehow do have direct epistemological access to God. If theology is about understanding God, how would we ever, in this life, figure out how close to the real God our linguistic accounts of God actually are? Where do we point to God to serve as a measuring device for how accurate our statements about God are? Moreover, for me, the term "understand" when applied to God may be mistakenly taken to be equivalent to "comprehending" God, and as the word "comprehend" connotes "encompassing" (from the Latin, after all, for "to grasp"), that implies that we human beings, by our theological reflection on our faith, actually may succeed in encompassing, grasping, or possessing God, and I find that a problematic, indeed idolatrous, notion. Second, although theological reflection may be considered by some to be itself an act of faith, it need not be. To say that theology is talk about God or that theological education must be about understanding God presupposes a belief in God, and not just as an assumption for the sake of the practice. It implies to me that people who don't believe God exists cannot produce decent theology, and I know from experience that is not true. I have known agnostics and even atheists who make, in my opinion, quite good theologians. I have known Jews who are good at Christian theology—without themselves believing in its claims. In the end, I think the only really defensible claim for theology, at least this side of the veil, is that it is critical reflection on the language and practices of faith, not that it is itself truly talk about God.

3. I grew up in Texas in Churches of Christ, which share a broader history with the Disciples of Christ (Christian Church) and independent Christian churches in what has been called "the Restoration Movement" or "the Stone-Campbell Movement." For histories of the movement, see David Edwin Harrell, *A Social History of the Disciples of Christ*, 2 vols. (Nashville: Disciples of Christ Historical Society, 1966–73); Nathan O. Hatch, *The Democratization of American Christianity* (New Haven, CT: Yale University Press, 1989); Richard T. Hughes, *Reviving the Ancient Faith: The Story of Churches of Christ in America* (Grand Rapids: Wm. B. Eerdmans, 1996); Henry E. Webb, *In Search of Christian Unity: A History of the Restoration Movement*, rev. ed. (Abilene, TX: ACU Press, 2003).

4. Bart D. Ehrman, *Misquoting Jesus: The Story behind Who Changed the Bible and Why* (San Francisco: HarperSanFrancisco, 2005), 7.

5. Even pronouncements by Roman Catholic hierarchy and councils that the Latin Vulgate is the *editio typica* for official use in Catholic churches do not identify only the Vulgate as Scripture. See "Vulgate," in *New Catholic Encyclopedia*, 2nd ed. (Washington, DC: Catholic University of America; Farmington Hills, MI: Thomson Gale, 2003), 14.591–600.

6. Some Christians have designated the physical, socially delineable institution(s) as "the visible church" and the full, unseen body of Christ as "the invisible church." But Christian theologians, at least many of them, prefer not to speak of the local congregation as the "visible church" and the entire body of Christ as the "invisible church," because, for one thing, as David Kelsey has put it, "the church universal is as concretely actual as is any local congregation" (Kelsey, *To Understand God Truly*, 149).

7. Again, Kelsey: "The greater church, with which particular congregations are in some way 'one,' that is, the church 'catholic' or 'ecumenical,' while always necessarily localizable, always present as particular congregations—though not necessarily *only* present as local congregations (whether or not it is present in other ways can remain an open question)—is never local*ized*, never exhaustively present as nor simply identical with a local congregation" (*To Understand God Truly*, 150–51).

8. The point is well made by Mark Jordan when speaking about Thomas Aquinas's beliefs about translation of Scripture: "Thomas's confidence in the possibility of translation is a theological confidence. It extends just to the essentials of faith. . . . It must be possible to articulate truths essential to faith in every language" (Mark D. Jordan, *Rewritten Theology: Aquinas after His Readers* [Malden, MA; Oxford; Carlton, Victoria, Australia: Blackwell, 2006], 26, 27).

9. The usually cited impulse for narrative theology and its understanding of Scripture as narrative is Frei, *Eclipse of Biblical Narrative*, mentioned above; but now there are hundreds of books and many more articles on the theme. Kelsey (*To Understand God Truly*, 170–71) explicitly makes the points I have highlighted here: that the other genres of Scripture are often taken by Christians as imbedded within the major, larger narratives that Christian Scripture is thought to contain.

10. For a fuller treatment of these ideas, see my *Sex and the Single Savior*, 170–81.

11. Don Browning, *Fundamental Practical Theology: Descriptive and Strategic Proposals* (Minneapolis: Fortress, 1991).

12. Interview with author, March 27, 2006.

13. Charles H. Cosgrove, *Appealing to Scripture in Moral Debate: Five Hermeneutical Rules* (Grand Rapids and Cambridge: Wm. B. Eerdmans, 2002), 9.

14. Ibid., 12; see, for these examples, 27–28, 34–37.

15. Ibid., 36–37. Numbers in subsequent paragraphs indicate page references in Cosgrove.

16. On Bernard, see ibid., 155–56. Cosgrove is quoting Wilfred Cantwell Smith, *What Is Scripture? A Comparative Approach* (Minneapolis: Fortress, 1993), 32.

17. Louisville, KY: Westminster John Knox, 2006.

18. Several recent studies have pointed to improvisation, either in music or in theater, as a way to think about theological reasoning. See, for example, Shannon Craigo-Snell, "Command Performance: Rethinking Performance Interpretation in the Context of *Divine Discourse*," *Modern Theology* 16 (2000): 475–94; Samuel Wells, *Improvisation: The Drama of Christian Ethics* (Grand Rapids: Brazos, 2004); A. K. M. Adam, "Poaching on Zion: Biblical Theology as Signifying Practice," in A. K. M. Adam, Stephen E. Fowl, Kevin J. Vanhoozer, and Francis Watson, *Reading Scripture with the Church: Toward a Hermeneutic for Theological Interpretation* (Grand Rapids: Baker Academic, 2006), 17–34, esp. 31; and several previous studies cited by these authors.

19. A good example is provided by Thomas H. Troeger, though he is illustrating how he uses his imagination to invent and compose a sermon. See *Imagining a Sermon* (Nashville: Abingdon, 1990), esp. 13–31. Appropriately, Troeger repeatedly uses the term "training the imagination." For another use of "imagination" in theology, here in direct reference to interpretation of Scripture, see Luke Timothy Johnson, "Imagining the World Scripture Imagines," *Modern Theology* 14 (1998): 165–80; also found in Johnson and William S. Kurz, *The Future of Catholic Biblical Scholarship: A Constructive Conversation* (Grand Rapids: Eerdmans, 2002),

119–42. One problem I have with Johnson's suggestions is his repeated claim that it is Scripture itself that "imagines" a "world." He may mean this as a metaphor. But if Johnson really believes that the world he believes is "imagined by scripture" is really "in" Scripture (rather than the result of human interpretation), his formulations, in my opinion, are misleading and false—and dangerously so. Such formulations, again, tend to mask the very real human agency necessary for any construction of a "world" thought to be represented in or by Scripture.

20. In an important recent study of the history of theologies of Scripture in Anglicanism, Rowan Greer shows how Anglican divines regularly were willing to agree with more rigorous Protestant reformers that Scripture may be said to be "infallible," but they added to that statement of faith the observation that all human interpretations of Scripture are indeed fallible. John Locke, for instance, "points out that the immense number of differing interpretations of the New Testament prove that, however infallible we suppose the text, [here quoting Locke] 'the reader may be, nay cannot choose but to be very fallible in the understanding of it.'" See Greer, *Anglican Approaches to Scripture*, 78. Anglican theologians repeatedly emphasized the necessity of interpretation, and its fallibility (see also xvi, 11, 15, 17, 29, 30, et passim). Much of the modern argument about whether or not the Bible is "infallible" would be moot if people recognized that human interpretation is always necessary, and even if one believes, in faith, that Scripture is "infallible"—meaning that it will not lead Christians to perdition or damning error—we may never claim "infallibility" for our own, very human interpretations. And no meaning of Scripture is available to us without human interpretation.

Chapter 5

1. Kelsey, *To Understand God Truly*, 15.
2. Several studies of theological schools have made this point. See the works cited in note 5 of chap. 1 above.
3. R. W. Southern, *Scholastic Humanism and the Unification of Europe*, vol. 1, *Foundations* (Oxford UK, and Cambridge, MA: Blackwell, 1995), 102.
4. Jean Leclercq, *The Love of Learning and the Desire for God: A Study of Monastic Culture*, trans. Catharine Misrahi (New York: Fordham University Press, 1982). 71. See also Lesley Smith, "Use of Scripture in Teaching at the Medieval University," 229–43; Lesley Smith, "What Was the Bible in the Twelfth and Thirteenth Centuries?" in *Neue Richtungen in der hoch- und spätmittelalterlichen Bibelexegese*, ed. Robert E. Lerner, 1–15 (Munich: R. Oldenbourg, 1996), 1–15. The point is made by several authors in Thomas J. Heffernan and Thomas E. Burman, eds., *Scripture and Pluralism: Reading the Bible in the Religiously Plural Worlds of the Middle Ages and Renaissance* (Leiden: Brill, 2005), esp. 74, 143–91.
5. Quoted by Greer in Kugel and Greer, *Early Biblical Interpretation*, 191. The quotation is from Cassian's *Conferences* 14.13. For the full text (in different translations), see Cassian, *Conferences*, trans. Colm Luibheid, or Cassian, *The Conferences*, trans. and annotated by Boniface Ramsey.
6. Kugel and Greer, *Early Biblical Interpretation*, 191.
7. Douglas Burton-Christie, *The Word in the Desert: Scripture and the Quest for Holiness in Early Christian Monasticism* (New York and Oxford: Oxford University Press, 1993), 117.
8. R. W. Southern, *Scholastic Humanism and the Unification of Europe*, vol. 2, *The Heroic Age* (Oxford: Blackwell, 2001), 12.

9. For some basic introductions to *lectio divina*, see M. Basil Pennington, *Lectio Divina: Renewing the Ancient Practice of Praying the Scriptures* (New York: Crossroad, 1998); along with his more simple, devotional handbook on centering prayer: M. Basil Pennington, *An Invitation to Centering Prayer* (Liguori, MO: Liguori, 2001). For a fuller introduction to *lectio divina*, including more historical contextualization of the practice, see Michael Casey, *Sacred Reading: The Ancient Art of Lectio Divina* (Liguori, MO: Triumph Books, 1996). For more on centering prayer: Thomas Keating, *Foundations for Centering Prayer and the Christian Contemplative Life* (New York: Continuum, 2002).

10. Perhaps I should remind the reader that I believe it is perfectly fine to speak about authors' intentions ("what Paul wanted to say") and to use metaphors of textual agency ("Scripture teaches us . . . ," "The passage says . . ."). The point I have tried to make in many different contexts is that such metaphorical expressions about textual agency or authorial intentions are dangerous only when they mislead us into forgetting about or hiding the interpretive agency of ourselves or other readers. In fact, it would be nigh impossible to avoid using all kinds of metaphors about texts and authors. My point is just that when we do so, we should remember that they are metaphors and that the text is not itself simply dispensing the meaning we see in it.

11. For example, even those churches that think of themselves as biblical rather than creedal usually assume the doctrine of the Trinity, which is a doctrine difficult to find in the Bible read literally and historically. Whether those churches realize it or not, many of their beliefs about the Trinity or the nature of Christ and the Holy Spirit come from Christian traditions, as embodied for instance in the creeds, rather than directly from the Bible.

Bibliography

Adam, A. K. M. *Faithful Interpretation: Reading the Bible in a Postmodern World*. Minneapolis: Fortress, 2006.

———. "Poaching on Zion: Biblical Theology as Signifying Practice." In *Reading Scripture with the Church: Toward a Hermeneutic for Theological Interpretation*, A. K. M. Adam, Stephen E. Fowl, Kevin J. Vanhoozer, and Francis Watson, 17–34. Grand Rapids: Baker Academic, 2006.

———. *What Is Postmodern Biblical Criticism?* Minneapolis: Fortress, 1995.

Aelred of Rievaulx. *Sermones inediti B. Aelredi Abbatis Rievallensis*. Edited by C. H. Talbot. Series scriptorum S. Ordinis Cisterciensis 1. Rome: Curiam Generalem Sacri Ordinis Cisterciensis, 1952.

Astell, Ann W. *The Song of Songs in the Middle Ages*. Ithaca, NY: Cornell University Press, 1990.

Augustine. *The Confessions*. Trans. Maria Boulding. Preface by Patricia Hampi. New York: Vintage, 1998.

Barr, James. *The Scope and Authority of the Bible*. Philadelphia: Westminster, 1980.

Bede, The Venerable. *Commentary on the Acts of the Apostles*. Trans. with an introduction and notes by Lawrence T. Martin. Kalamazoo, MI: Cistercian, 1989.

Bernard of Clairvaux. *On the Song of Songs, Sermones super Cantica Canticorum*. Trans. Kilian Walsh. Introduction by Corneille Halfants. 4 vols. Spencer, MA: Cistercian, 1971–1980.

Browning, Don. *Fundamental Practical Theology: Descriptive and Strategic Proposals*. Minneapolis: Fortress, 1991.

Brueggemann, Walter. *Theology of the Old Testament: Testimony, Dispute, Advocacy*. Minneapolis: Fortress, 1997.

Burton-Christie, Douglas. *The Word in the Desert: Scripture and the Quest for Holiness in Early Christian Monasticism*. New York and Oxford: Oxford University Press, 1993.

Candler, Peter M., Jr. "St. Thomas Aquinas." In *Christian Theologies of Scripture: A Comparative Introduction*, Justin S. Holcomb, ed., 60–80. New York: New York University Press, 2006.

Carroll, Jackson W., Barbara G. Wheeler, Daniel O. Aleshire, and Penny Long Marler. *Being There: Culture and Formation in Two Theological Schools*. New York and Oxford: Oxford University Press, 1997.

Casey, Michael. *Sacred Reading: The Ancient Art of Lectio Divina*. Liguori, MO: Triumph Books, 1996.

Clark, Elizabeth A. *History, Theory, Text: Historians and the Linguistic Turn*. Cambridge, MA: Harvard University Press, 2004.

Cosgrove, Charles H. *Appealing to Scripture in Moral Debate: Five Hermeneutical Rules*. Grand Rapids and Cambridge: Wm. B. Eerdmans, 2002.

Craigo-Snell, Shannon. "Command Performance: Rethinking Performance Interpretation in the Context of *Divine Discourse*." *Modern Theology* 16 (2000): 475–94.

Culler, Jonathan. "Making Sense." *Twentieth-Century Studies* 12 (1974): 27–36.

Dyck, Elmer, ed. *The Act of Bible Reading: A Multidisciplinary Approach to Biblical Interpretation*. Downers Grove, IL: InterVarsity, 1996.

Ehrman, Bart D. *Misquoting Jesus: The Story behind Who Changed the Bible and Why*. San Francisco: HarperSanFrancisco, 2005.

Farley, Edward. *The Fragility of Knowledge: Theological Education in the Church and the University*. Philadelphia: Fortress, 1988.

———. *Theologia: The Fragmentation and Unity of Theological Education*. Philadelphia: Fortress, 1983.

Fish, Stanley. *Doing What Comes Naturally: Change, Rhetoric, and the Practice of Theory in Literary and Legal Studies*. Durham, NC: Duke University Press, 1989.

———. *Is There a Text in This Class? The Authority of Interpretive Communities*. Cambridge, MA: Harvard University Press, 1980.

Foster, Charles R., Lisa E. Dahill, Lawrence A. Golemon, and Barbara Wang Tolentino. *Educating Clergy: Teaching Practices and Pastoral Imagination*. San Francisco: Jossey-Bass, 2006.

Frei, Hans W. *The Eclipse of Biblical Narrative: A Study in Eighteenth- and Nineteenth-Century Hermeneutics*. New Haven, CT: Yale University Press, 1974.

———. *The Identity of Jesus Christ: The Hermeneutical Bases of Dogmatic Theology*. Philadelphia: Fortress, 1975.

Greer, Rowan A. *Anglican Approaches to Scripture: From the Reformation to the Present*. New York: Crossroad, 2006.

Greer, Rowan A., and Margaret M. Mitchell. *The "Belly-Myther" of Endor: Interpretations of 1 Kingdoms 28 in the Early Church*. Atlanta: Society of Biblical Literature, 2007.

Harrell, David Edwin. *A Social History of the Disciples of Christ*. 2 vols. Nashville: Disciples of Christ Historical Society, 1966–73.

Hatch, Nathan O. *The Democratization of American Christianity*. New Haven, CT: Yale University Press, 1989.

Hays, Richard B. *The Moral Vision of the New Testament: Community, Cross, New Creation: A Contemporary Introduction to New Testament Ethics*. San Francisco: HarperSanFrancisco, 1996.

Heffernan, Thomas J., and Thomas E. Burman, eds. *Scripture and Pluralism: Reading the Bible in the Religiously Plural Worlds of the Middle Ages and Renaissance*. Leiden: Brill, 2005.

Holcomb, Justin S., ed. *Christian Theologies of Scripture: A Comparative Introduction*. New York: New York University Press, 2006.

Hough, Joseph C., and John B. Cobb. *Christian Identity and Theological Education*. Atlanta: Scholars Press, 1985.

Hughes, Richard T. *Reviving the Ancient Faith: The Story of Churches of Christ in America*. Grand Rapids: Wm. B. Eerdmans, 1996.

Jenkins, Keith. *Re-thinking History: With a New Preface and Conversation with the Author by Alun Munslow*. London: Routledge, 2003.

John Cassian. *Conferences*. Trans. Colm Luibheid. New York: Paulist, 1985.

———. *The Conferences*. Trans. and annotated by Boniface Ramsey. New York: Paulist, 1997.

Johnson, Luke Timothy. "Imagining the World Scripture Imagines." *Modern Theology* 14 (1998): 165–80.

Johnson, Luke Timothy, and William S. Kurz. *The Future of Catholic Biblical Scholarship: A Constructive Conversation*. Grand Rapids: Eerdmans, 2002.

Jordan, Mark D. *Rewritten Theology: Aquinas after His Readers*. Malden, MA; Oxford; Carlton, Victoria, Australia: Blackwell, 2006.

Keating, Thomas. *Foundations for Centering Prayer and the Christian Contemplative Life*. New York: Continuum, 2002.

Kelsey, David H. *To Understand God Truly: What's Theological about a Theological School*. Louisville, KY: Westminster/John Knox, 1992.

———. *The Uses of Scripture in Recent Theology*. Philadelphia: Fortress, 1985. Revised and republished as *Proving Doctrine: The Uses of Scripture in Modern Theology*. Harrisburg, PA: Trinity Press International, 1999.

Kugel, James L., and Rowan A. Greer. *Early Biblical Interpretation*. Library of Early Christianity. Philadelphia: Westminster, 1986.

Leclercq, Jean. *The Love of Learning and the Desire for God: A Study of Monastic Culture*. Translated by Catharine Misrahi. New York: Fordham University Press, 1982.

Lienhard, Joseph T., trans. *Origen: Homilies on Luke; and, Fragments on Luke*. The Fathers of the Church 94. Washington, DC: Catholic University of America Press, 1996.

Lindbeck, George A. *The Nature of Doctrine: Religion and Theology in a Postliberal Age*. Philadelphia: Westminster, 1984.

Martin, Dale B. *Sex and the Single Savior: Gender and Sexuality in Biblical Interpretation*. Louisville, KY: Westminster John Knox, 2006.

McKenzie, Steven L., and Stephen R. Haynes, eds. *To Each Its Own Meaning: An Introduction to Biblical Criticisms and Their Application*. Rev. and expanded. Louisville, KY: Westminster John Knox, 1999.

Mitchell, Margaret M. "Patristic Rhetoric on Allegory: Origen and Eustathius Put 1 Samuel 28 on Trial." *The Journal of Religion* 85 (2005): 414–45.

Mudflower Collective, The. *God's Fierce Whimsy: Christian Feminism and Theological Education*. New York: Pilgrim, 1985.

Pennington, M. Basil. *An Invitation to Centering Prayer*. Liguori, MO: Liguori, 2001.

———. *Lectio Divina: Renewing the Ancient Practice of Praying the Scriptures*. New York: Crossroad, 1998.

Preus, James Samuel. *From Shadow to Promise: Old Testament Interpretation from Augustine to the Young Luther*. Cambridge, MA: Harvard University Press, 1969.

Rogers, Jack. *Jesus, the Bible, and Homosexuality: Explode the Myths, Heal the Church*. Louisville, KY: Westminster John Knox, 2006.

Roncace, Mark, and Patrick Gray. *Teaching the Bible: Practical Strategies for Classroom Instruction*. Leiden and Boston: Brill, 2005.

Smalley, Beryl. *The Study of the Bible in the Middle Ages*. 3rd ed., rev. Oxford: Blackwell, 1983.

Smith, Jonathan Z. *Drudgery Divine: On the Comparison of Early Christianities and the Religions of Late Antiquity*. Chicago: Chicago University Press, 1990.

Smith, Lesley. "The Use of Scripture in Teaching at the Medieval University." In *Learning Institutionalized: Teaching in the Medieval University*, edited by John van Engen, 229–43. Notre Dame, IN: University of Notre Dame Press, 2000.

———. "What Was the Bible in the Twelfth and Thirteenth Centuries?" In *Neue Richtungen in der hoch- und spätmittelalterlichen Bibelexegese*, edited by Robert E. Lerner, 1–15. Munich: R. Oldenbourg, 1996.

Smith, Wilfred Cantwell. *What Is Scripture? A Comparative Approach*. Minneapolis: Fortress, 1993.

Southern, R. W. *Scholastic Humanism and the Unification of Europe*. Vol. 1, *Foundations*. Oxford, UK, and Cambridge, MA: Blackwell, 1995.

———. *Scholastic Humanism and the Unification of Europe*. Vol. 2, *The Heroic Age*. Oxford: Blackwell, 2001.

Squire, Aelred. *Aelred of Rievaulx: A Study*. Kalamazoo, MI: Cistercian Publications, 1981.

Stanley, Christopher D. *Arguing with Scripture: The Rhetoric of Quotations in the Letters of Paul*. New York: T. & T. Clark, 2004.

———. *Paul and the Language of Scripture: Citation Technique in the Pauline Epistles and Contemporary Literature*. Cambridge: Cambridge University Press, 1992.

Thomas Aquinas. *Commentary on the Gospel of St. John*. Trans. James A. Weisheipl with Fabian R. Larcher. Aquinas Scripture Series. Vol. 4, pt. 1. Albany, NY: Magi, 1980.

Troeger, Thomas H. *Imagining a Sermon*. Nashville: Abingdon, 1990.

Vanhoozer, Kevin J. "The Reader in New Testament Interpretation." In *Hearing the New Testament: Strategies for Interpretation*, edited by Joel B. Green, 301–28. Grand Rapids: Wm. B. Eerdmans, 1995.

Volf, Miroslav. "Theology for a Way of Life." In *Practicing Theology: Beliefs and Practices in Christian Life*, edited by Miroslav Volf and Dorothy C. Bass, 245–63. Grand Rapids: Eerdmans, 2002.

"Vulgate." In *New Catholic Encyclopedia*. 2nd ed., 14.591–600. Washington, DC: Catholic University of America; Farmington Hills, MI: Thomson Gale, 2003.

Webb, Henry E. *In Search of Christian Unity: A History of the Restoration Movement*. Rev. ed. Abilene, TX: ACU Press, 2003.

Wells, Samuel. *Improvisation: The Drama of Christian Ethics*. Grand Rapids: Brazos, 2004.

Wiles, Maurice. *Maurice Wiles*. Explorations in Theology 4. London: SCM, 1979.

Wills, Garry. *Saint Augustine*. London: Orion House, 2000.

Wood, Charles M. *Vision and Discernment: An Orientation in Theological Study*. Atlanta: Scholars Press, 1985.

Wright, N. T. *The Last Word: Beyond the Bible Wars to a New Understanding of the Authority of Scripture*. San Francisco: HarperSanFrancisco, 2005.

Young, Frances. "Allegory and the Ethics of Reading." In *Open Text: New Dimensions for Biblical Studies?* edited by Francis Watson, 103–20. London: SCM, 1993.

Scripture Index

Author and Subject Index